EMPOWERING INTUITIVES

A SPIRITUAL TOOL KIT FOR THE MODERN WORLD

REV. DR. MICHELLE WALKER, DNP

Virginia

Published in the United States by WriteLife Publishing

(An imprint of Boutique of Quality Books Publishing Company, Inc.)
www.writelife.com

Printed in the United States of America

978-1-60808-243-8 (p)
978-1-60808-244-5 (e)

Library of Congress Control Number 2020947711

Book design by Robin Krauss, www.bookformatters.com
Cover design by Rebecca Lown, www.rebeccalowndesign.com
First editor: Allison Itterly
Second editor: Andrea Berns

PRAISE FOR EMPOWERING INTUITIVES
AND
DR. MICHELLE WALKER

"Michelle has composed a lively and readable text with simple and easy-to-use exercises, many of which are especially accessible to children that help them to tap their own intuitive abilities with ease. This simple volume of spiritual wisdom brings together centuries of timeless knowledge into an easy-to-use compendium that someone can take, from day one, and move towards greater knowledge of one's self and one's place in the cosmos in one evening. Dr. Walker is a gifted intuitive and medium and her warmth and kindness pervades every page of text."

– Chris Bennett, CRNP

". . . As a clinician, I highly recommend this book to anyone in helping professions or doing light work with clients. The practical exercises in this book will help professionals create a well-organized self-care routine to avoid burn-out and compassion fatigue. However, because this book is easy to follow and the concepts are presented in a very simple and logical way, it also makes a great tool to use with clients of all ages, including children."

– Angela House, LCSW-C, CCTP, RMT

"Being a skeptic, you have to admit there are things that cannot be explained. When those things happen, whom do you turn to for answers? How do you know you're not getting some hocus-pocus answer from someone? Dr. Michelle Walker is a highly intuitive medium who has years of experience and an endless library of knowledge in the metaphysical world. Her accuracy turned me from a stubborn skeptic to an open-minded human being. Michelle is my go-to intuitive for all my spiritual needs. I highly recommend her to everyone."

– Kelly Van Fleet

"Dr. Michelle Walker has been my spiritual mentor for years. Since we've connected, my life has been upgraded in ways I would not have even imagined. I have been a student in her intuitive development class for about two years. Dr. Michelle is an excellent teacher and my intuition has developed remarkably. I have seen my growth weekly with the instructions she gives to help me open my senses to receive spiritual insight. This woman is incredible, and her class is amazing. I love her and the students who attend; we've grown bonds that will last forever. Thank you so much, Dr. Michelle, for being my soul sister and creating our tribe. I love you forever!"

– Jocelynn Jones

"My reading with Michelle was highly accurate and helped me to make a very important decision. My situation was work related and with her guidance, I was able to gain knowledge and peace. She precisely described the person I was dealing with as if she knew them personally. Michelle is not only able to provide insight and readings, but her personality is angelic, spreading such peace and light. She is definitely graced with a gift from God."

– Courtney Tashko, CRNP

"Michelle's book is both inspiring and practical. In her compelling story she shares her intimate experiences with spiritual guidance and how she chose to use her God given gifts in a practical way throughout her life that are easy to relate to. The exercises in this book provide us with easy to use tools to enhance what each of us is born with and a wealth of resources to explore in her footnotes. I thoroughly enjoyed her story which was hard to put down and the exercises are precise, easy to do, and produce the intended results."

– Rev. Elaine D. Thomas, MS,
Director, Fellowships of the Spirit

To my soul family on both sides of the veil for the unwavering love and support to facilitate this book. I am grateful for *God and all of the guides, angels, teachers, and fellow light* workers who continue to anchor the divine light and for supporting me along this journey.

TABLE OF CONTENTS

INTRODUCTION

I am a natural-born intuitive or empath and use these terms interchangeably in this book. I have struggled my entire life to understand my intuitive abilities and mediumship while trying to find a balance walking in both the spiritual and physical worlds. When I was three years old, I had a traumatic experience, and what was birthed from that experience was seeing my first full apparition of an angel. I was lying in bed, and the angel put his hand on my shoulder and said, "Stay here." Then I heard voices shouting from the hallway. When I got up to see what was happening, the angel blocked the doorway so I couldn't pass, and then he hugged and comforted me until the voices stopped. I told my mother about it, but she just brushed it off as having an active imagination. It was difficult to wrap my head around what I had seen and experienced when the adults in my life didn't believe me. Being able to see an angel so clearly felt comforting, but I didn't understand why I was the only one who could see him. That was my first visual experience, but I've had many throughout the years. As an adult, I came to the realization that I needed to nurture these visuals, that these divine spirits were here to help me, so I sought out many mentors, read countless books, and I have learned to trust the divine spirits who are guiding my life.

My experiences led to the development of this book to serve as a basis for understanding your own innate abilities and in the hopes to assist you in finding a workable balance. I came by this information through my life experiences and in communicating with Spirit. Throughout this book, I refer to "Spirit" as the divine beings I communicate with. I recognize that everyone has their own spiritual and religious beliefs, so Spirit can include, but is not limited to, God, archangels, angels, ascended masters, guardians, spirit guides, and spirit loved ones. "My spiritual team," as I like to call them, is a collective counsel that brings forth guidance for me in all aspects of my life. They work alongside me in my personal life, my work as a DNP (Doctor of Nursing Practice), and in my ministry as a medical intuitive and Spiritualist Reverend. I provide care in a family practice, as well as counseling, psychic mediumship readings, and facilitate students in a weekly developmental circle as part of my ministry.

My work is focused to help balance the body, mind, and spirit for total healing using my education and trainings in both Eastern and Western medicine and modalities and intuitive abilities. In a world with so much uncertainty, unrest, fear, and hate, we should begin to look inward to our spirit team that guides us to find what we seek outside of ourselves. In *The Wizard of Oz*, Glinda the Good Witch says to Dorothy, "You always had the power, my dear, you just had to learn it for yourself."[1] This is the best way to describe how we come to trust and understand our world and intuitive abilities. We are born with them, and as we navigate our experiences, we first ask our parents then our friends and teachers, bosses, and religious leaders who help us in our lives. But then there comes a time when no one seems to have the entire answer, which lights the fire for our self-discovery.

I recall just before my eleventh birthday that I was seeking to understand the life-and-death circle after one of my close friends committed suicide earlier that year. This led me to question my Lutheran upbringing when I did not receive an answer that was satisfactory from my minister. I researched other religions, and

1 *The Wizard of Oz*, DVD, directed by Victor Fleming (1939, Culver City, CA: Warner Home Video, 2013).

while some of what they said overlapped and made sense, nothing felt completely accurate. I explored the possibility of everything being predestined, which led me to find Nostradamus and Socrates. This opened up Pandora's Box. For a year or so, I was having premonitions of events before they occurred, and I finally felt like I understood that I was not making things happen and that people can receive such information. I just didn't understand how, exactly. It was complicated reading for a middle-schooler, but the drive and desire to understand my "special gifts" compelled me to read more and understand. What I later discovered was that I was coming into my puberty years where my visions and psychic abilities would be developing and opening up more frequently.

One night before my twelfth birthday, I was awoken by a woman's voice calling my name and a beautiful white light shining around the cracks of my bedroom door. Then a beautiful woman appeared in my doorway. I did not recognize her, but it felt like I knew her, as there was something familiar about her.

"Hello, Michelle," she said. "I'm Mary, your grandmother."

I wasn't scared, and I felt comforted by her presence. She told me that she had been assisting me with my psychic abilities since birth and that things were going to get intense. She sat on my bed, and we talked for what seemed like hours.

I had never met my grandmother Mary in life because she passed into spirit before I was born. She was also intuitive, and I had a lot of her mannerisms, from what other family members have told me. I was a bit skeptical, so I asked, "How can I be sure that you are who you say you are?"

My grandmother smiled. "Go into your mother's cedar chest in her bedroom. You'll find the answer there."

The next day, I snuck into my mother's bedroom when my mother was at work. The cedar chest was in the back corner of her closet and full of photo albums. Inside, there was one picture of my grandmother when she was sick right before her death. Though it barely looked like the woman who had visited me, my grandfather was standing beside her bed in the photo, and I knew it was her. That was the proof I needed to begin to trust and understand my spirit team. This is why I believe Spirit sent my grandmother to be the one to speak to me, as I knew her energy and would want to have some tangible proof.

The world can be difficult to navigate without a firm, solid foundation for us to trust and rely on. For me, there never seemed to be that stability in the outside world, so I began to trust my spirit team. I grew up in an environment where the paranormal experience caused intense fear, and I was told not to discuss it because people would think I was "crazy" for predicting events and lock me away. When the environment was too harsh for me and I needed an escape to isolate by myself, I was considered *sensitive* and *emotional*.

As an empath, it can be hard to be around certain situations, such as watching horror movies or people being abused or hurt, because I will feel what they are experiencing in my own body. I am hypersensitive to the energy in a room, a person, or a situation, which can be difficult to stay calm and in my own space. If someone is upset, grieving, or yelling, it is hard for me to not let that person's energy overcome my own. How do you feel when someone yells at you? Do you feel the intensity of their words and emotions? As an empath, you cannot help but feel that energy in your physical body until you learn how to manage your energy. You can feel overwhelmed by other people's energies and carry their issues on your own shoulders as the weight of the world with no way to let it go. This can cause unhealed emotional issues that will need to be healed.

My goal in writing this book is to help, guide, illuminate, and allow you to gain the knowledge from my life experiences and Spirit guidance. My intention with this book is to help you understand your own abilities and how to strengthen them. I want you to learn how to work with your spiritual team to gain a higher understanding of this world and how to manage your feelings and your perspective to become the best version of yourself. I believe that we have the power to heal any issues we may have created, intentionally or unintentionally, through our life experiences by utilizing all the tools we have at our disposal. And when we cannot find the answers, we must learn to go within to receive guidance from the spirit world.

As an empathic being trying to navigate this world, I completely understand the challenge it is to successfully cope and grow on a spiritual path. I see so many people, especially children, struggle to understand their intuitive natures and how to incorporate them into their lives. Though there is more acceptance in today's world for those of us with these strong gifts, it is still challenging to navigate the emotional rollercoaster of self-acceptance and embracing our authentic selves. Assisting others on their path is my pleasure and passion.

In this book, you will discover and identify the traits of highly intuitive people. Each chapter provides self-discovery questions that will assist you in identifying blocks and opening up your connection with your spirit. I discuss in depth the many ways you can develop your own psychic abilities. I have also provided ways to help you understand how your mind works and how intentions create your reality, which is the key to changing your life. Once I gained this knowledge, it became a game changer. I was no longer the victim of my life circumstances or past experiences. It was excitingly mind-blowing to learn that I have the power to change my mindset and that Spirit is my guiding force. You will discover ways to shift your mindsets and perhaps your life.

At the end of each chapter, there are exercises to assist in strengthening your spiritual muscles. Though it is not required, I recommend keeping a journal so you can keep track of your experiences and progress. As always, check with your healthcare provider before trying any of these exercises to ensure they are appropriate for you or your loved ones.

I am so happy to share my journey with you, and I hope that you will relate to similar experiences in your own life. Through practicing the exercises, you can strengthen your intuition, as I provide new tools to use in your daily life. I encourage you to keep an open mind and explore the various aspects of this book so you may gain a deeper perspective of how you are living in this modern world.

CHAPTER 1

INTUITIVES

When I was in my mid-twenties, I went through a huge life transformation. I wanted a change in my environment and to make a fresh start with my son after my divorce. I was fresh out of nursing school, so I found a nursing position near a beach in Florida. I interviewed and was offered a position. I found a place to stay and was a few weeks from moving when I started to have strong gut feelings of doubt about whether I should go. I chalked up these feelings to nerves and pushed them aside. But ignoring my feelings never works if it is a sign from Spirit, and in this case, those feelings worsened dramatically. I was literally sick to my stomach, having heart palpitations and feelings of dread. At that time, I was very stubborn and did not easily follow Spirit's signs and messages.

One night, I heard a voice say, "Do not go . . . now is not the time." It was a male voice as clear as day. I decided to listen to the voice and changed my plans to move. Later that week, I received a call that the townhouse where I signed the lease had significant water damage from a recent storm. Then I got a call from the employer stating there was an issue, which would cause a delay in me starting the position. And what do you know? I was offered an even better job at my current employer and reconnected with a wonderful man. This is just one way that Spirit is looking out for our highest good and keeping us out of harm's way.

My reason for bringing up that experience is to highlight what it means to be an intuitive. What is an *intuitive*? An intuitive person is someone who often sees, feels, senses, or hears things that others do not. What an intuitive experiences tells him or her more about their environment and the people in it than words ever could. My belief is that we are *all* intuitive whether or not we acknowledge it or use it.

Intuition is our divine birthright that allows for a direct connection between Spirit to work in us and through us. Everyone has an ego, which is our conscious mind. Your intuition, however, goes deeper than your conscious mind and is your link to your higher self. In fact, it's even deeper than your subconscious. For the purposes of this book, I will refer to this as the *intuitive mind*.

When we are honoring and acknowledging our intuition, we become more self-aware, and we begin to work with one foot in the conscious mind and the other foot in the intuitive mind. From this intuitive bridge, you can channel divine impressions, visions, messages, and knowledge, and anchor them into the present conscious mind.

Learning to differentiate the subtle differences between the ego and the intuitive mind is the key. Throughout this book, you will learn how to use these subtle skills to help yourself and others.

Every day, we are faced with many choices such as what to wear, what to eat, and what to do in our spare time. We are also faced with more difficult choices, such as confronting a coworker or having a meaningful conversation with a friend who has hurt us. As humans with egos, we tend to read into things, but there are certain things that require us to dive a little deeper. Using your intuitive mind allows you to tap into your compassion and empathy for others, whereas using the ego mind focuses solely on yourself and your perspective. Do you honor the intuitive mind? Do you rationalize your issue or problem and allow the ego mind to run through the list of shoulds (i.e., *I should be polite, I should not judge, I should allow myself time to make a decision*), which would validate your initial intuitive feeling? Those who trust their intuition can navigate around a lot of unnecessary experiences.

Some believe that intuition is our most valuable asset. Steve Jobs described intuition as "more powerful than intellect."[2] Throughout history and in every culture, the communication of our intuition happens repeatedly in ways that current science can't explain. Intuition's most important role is that it alerts us to the path, people, and circumstances that we will uniquely find fulfilling. Once thought of as woo-woo performed by psychics and crystal-ball-viewing gypsies is now gaining the scientific rigor to validate intuitive experiences. Ivy Estabrooke, a program manager at the Office of Naval Research, said, "There is a growing body of anecdotal evidence, combined with solid research efforts, that suggests intuition is a critical aspect of how we humans interact with our environment and how, ultimately, we make many of our decisions."[3]

Have your gut instincts ever been so loud that you could not help but heed their warnings? That gut instinct—a sixth sense, an innate wisdom, an inner knowingness, or inner voice—often guides our decisions even if we are not conscious of it. Do your friends and family often come to you for advice because you "just know" about people or situations? Do you feel strongly about a person when you first meet them? Have you ever entered a new place and gotten the feeling that you needed to leave immediately? All of these are examples of your intuition, that unconscious reasoning

---

2 Jenny Medeiros, "Here's Why Steve Jobs Said Intuition is Absolutely More Powerful Than Intellect," Goalcast, June 26, 2018, https://www.goalcast.com/2018/06/26/steve-jobs-said-intuition-is-more-powerful-than-intellect/.

3 Channing Joseph, "U.S. Navy Program to Study How Troops Use Intuition," *New York Times*, March 27, 2012, https://atwar.blogs.nytimes.com/2012/03/27/navy-program-to-study-how-troops-use-intuition/

propelling you to do or experience something without telling you the why or how.

I have experienced all of these things as far back as I can remember. While the advice or guidance was always correct, I may not have always listened, or I experienced less than desirable outcomes as I often see in my practice. I've worked in the healthcare field for twenty-three years, and I've been counseling clients for over eight years as a Spiritualist Reverend. When I ask people how and why they make decisions in their life, I find their answers fall into one of the three categories: (1) people follow, or don't follow, their gut, (2) things just magically align, or, (3) there's an unplanned serendipitous coincidence. Learning to read the signs both internally and externally from our bodies and life experiences strengthens our intuitive abilities and our overall human experiences.

According to *Oxford University Press*, the term *New Age* is defined as "a broad movement characterized by alternative approaches to traditional Western culture, with an interest in spirituality, mysticism, holism, and environmentalism."[4] In other words, New Age is about finding a spiritual practice that resonates with you and enables personal transformation and healing.

There are some common traits in highly intuitive people. Intuitives are often highly sensitive to the energy of others, environments, and the subtle changes within themselves. They can feel overwhelmed in large crowds and need to spend time alone. Intuitives often have very vivid dreams and remember them. They are "spot-on" in their interpretation of other people. For instance, intuitives will get red flags and intuitive feelings right away about someone and can see through a façade of charisma, beauty, and

---

4 *Lexico Online*, s.v. "New Age," accessed 2019, https://www.lexico.com/en/definition/new_age

superficial traits to sense the soul. But being intuitive goes deeper than just a "gut feeling."

Some intuitive people may fear their own abilities. For example, maybe you've seen something before it happened and that frightened you. Or maybe you were conditioned not to tell people your premonitions for fear of rejection or persecution from peers. For others, it may be the fear of the unknown. Maybe you were brought up in a highly religious household or a rational scientific household. If you are going to explore your intuition, you need to understand if you are experiencing fear and where it is coming from. All of this will be explored throughout this book. I believe everyone is intuitive and can learn to develop their abilities if they choose to. That being said, not everyone is meant to become a psychic medium in this lifetime, but they can learn to use their intuition to enhance whatever path they are on.

The terms *empath* and *intuitive* are interchangeable in this book. I describe an intuitive as someone whose nature is highly refined to be sensitive to energy and their surroundings. Empaths and intuitives are often used to explain the same abilities; however, a person can be one or the other or both in how they process information. An intuitive looks inside of themselves to seek knowledge and understanding with the assistance of Spirit. An empath gains information from their external environment sensing and interpreting the energies.

According to psychiatrist Dr. Judith Orloff, "When over-whelmed with the impact of stressful emotions, empaths can have panic attacks, depression, chronic fatigue, food, sex and drug binges, and many physical symptoms that defy traditional medical diagnosis."[5] An empathic person can learn to navigate this world differently through self-awareness, body scanning, and other

5 Judith Orloff, "The Top 10 Traits of an Empath," accessed May 26, 2020, https://drjudithorloff.com/top-10-traits-of-an-empath/.

tools in their spiritual toolbox. As with anything else, you need to identify it in order to work on it and through it.

I have experienced all of these things and more. It can be very challenging to understand and take control of your life experiences, but it's absolutely worth it. Once I gained an understanding of my thoughts, my words, my actions, and how they interplay with others, it changed my life. I learned how to sense energies outside of my body through hands-on therapy such as reiki, integrated energy therapy, Jin Shin Jyutsu, and qigong. I studied mediumship, philosophy, medical intuition, and other metaphysical topics, and I learned to go within and build a relationship with Spirit. Keeping a balance is every empath's struggle, which begins with self-awareness. But it didn't come easy. All throughout my childhood, I struggled with visions and voices, and I was both afraid and exhilarated by it all. As far back as three years old, I can remember talking with angels. As a child, I enjoyed spending time alone in the grass. I loved spending time outside where I could hear nature. It was all very comforting.

I always knew I was different from my peers and my siblings, and I felt like I didn't belong most of my life. I did not understand the games little girls played, like house and with baby dolls. I didn't even own a Barbie doll until I was in my thirties! I often played sports with the boys because it helped me get out of my mind and decreased the voices and visions. I talked with animals and felt I understood what they needed. I would bring home every stray or hurt animal and try to heal them. My neighbor, Bernie, was like a mother to me. She was always up for the challenge of whatever animal needed our help. She would listen to what I would tell her the animal needed.

I grew up in a single-mother household with my siblings. We did not have much communication on things like religion, life purpose, philosophy, or prophesy. Our house was more about survival, as my siblings and I were supervised but left on our own a lot of the time. There was much fear and resistance to questioning the norm. Questioning the norm was exactly what I did all the time because so much in my life did not make sense to what I was seeing and experiencing in the spirit world and in the physical world. I learned to not share with many people and to deal with grief and loss of loved ones on my own.

From the ages of ten through twenty-two, seven loved ones—family and close friends—passed into spirit, all of whom came to me in visions or dreams before they passed. I used to have a recurring vision or dream three times in a row, and on the third night was when they would pass. I remember when Bernie came to me and woke me out of my sleep to tell me she was in the hospital *dying and wanted to tell me she loved me. I was around thirteen* at the time. The next day, I went to her house and found out that Bernie was in the hospital in intensive care. I begged and pleaded with my mother to take me to see her in the hospital, but she refused. Hospitals would not allow children in intensive care units back then.

The next night in my dream, I saw Bernie in her coffin at the funeral home, and I awoke to her telling me that it was okay that I couldn't come to see her. She said that she loved every bit of this life with me. On the third night, I saw her standing beside my bed, then she kissed my forehead, waved goodbye, and lay down in the coffin. I found out later that she visited me at the exact time of her death. When I attended her funeral, she was lying in the coffin exactly as I had envisioned it.

The night after Bernie's funeral, I was lying in bed and saw the figure of a woman gliding across the ceiling and then floating toward the floor. She moved toward me, but I was not afraid, as I somehow "knew" her loving energy, but at the same time, I did not recognize her face. She was around seven feet tall with brown hair. She hugged me, which felt like pure love. It was cold energy, and my hair stood up, but it also felt like a big, warm hug and was so very calming. She sat with me for what seemed like hours, helping me understand some of the emotional things I was going through. She spoke to me just as I would sit and talk with anyone. She reassured me that things would work out and that I needed to let go of my fear and sadness around losing many people close to me.

"Your loved ones are still with you—always—helping and loving you," she said. I did not understand until years later that she was the spirit of one of my guardian angels, and she was in fact telling me the truth. Every time I have been in the presence of an angel, there is a silent, dense space. The closest thing I have come to this is parasailing one thousand feet in the air—there is just a peaceful silence.

That was such a profound moment in my life with Spirit as a teenager. I was so blessed to have been able to see, hear, and feel Bernie with me, yet so saddened to lose her and not be able to tell anyone about what I was experiencing. It was a time of great grief for me. I was raised Lutheran, so I asked God to not let me see anything anymore because it was too painful. I felt helpless but believed I was to help people somehow with my visions. As an adult, I learned that being able to help souls transition from this physical world to the spiritual world was one of the greatest things I could help them do, as well as to help their families understand the process from a unique perspective, which was one reason I entered the nursing field.

A big challenge for intuitives and empaths is to not shut down their abilities. After Bernie passed, I was completely overwhelmed with just the basic functions of life and felt like I'd lost the one person who understood me and my abilities and loved me completely. I suppressed my intuitive abilities as best I could and would tell them all to go away. A lot of people I have encountered have "shut down" their intuitive abilities due to trauma or negative conditioning. We can feel so much that our instinctive protective defenses push away the intuitive feelings and communication. It wasn't until I was an adult and had a near-death experience that everything shifted. I found myself along this spiritual path rediscovering my divine nature and abilities. I had an aha moment, a moment of clarity where everything made sense. My hope is that you are on that path of self-discovery and self-awareness. There is great strength in connecting with like-minded souls. Knowing you are not alone allows us to be vulnerable and share our loving souls.

I became a nurse twenty-three years ago to help others heal their body, mind, and spirit. I've worked in many fields: oncology, pediatrics, intensive care, hospice, rehabilitation, and long-term care. After thirteen years of being a nurse and assisting hundreds of souls to transition to the spirit world, I felt called to continue my Western education. I earned a Doctorate of Nursing Practice (DNP) degree. I work in public health serving families of all needs. I furthered my spiritual path as I returned to my studies five years ago as a Spiritualist Reverend, and I serve Spirit through my ministry with medical intuition and connecting clients with their spirit loved ones to facilitate healing on both sides.

Being an intuitive and an empath propelled me on this career path in the medical field and the spiritual field. But it all stemmed from when I was three years old, that little girl who saw visions and heard voices and felt so alone in the world. My story (unfortunately) is very similar to other empathic children who do not have other intuitives supporting and guiding their spiritual path. Childhood was a very scary and troubling time as I tried to make sense of these abilities and how to navigate them. This is one of the reasons I created this book, so I can help others like me find an easier way to embrace their divine gifts.

CHAPTER 2

SUBTLE ENERGY BODIES

Empaths use their intuition to gain understanding of people, places, and things whether aware of it or not. For example, you make an intuitive impression when you meet someone for the first time. You assess their appearance if they are clean, nicely dressed, or unkempt. You get a feeling regarding their personality traits if they are kind, arrogant, trustworthy, or knowledgeable. Assessing their energy can give you a feeling of loving, calm, joyful, sad, or scattered thoughts. These impressions occur within the first few minutes of interacting, and then you can decide how the interaction will proceed. If someone is in a sad, depressed state and needs a listening ear, you may decide to pull up a chair and listen. The opposite is true if you find the person to be yelling, angry, or even hostile, and you will most likely leave.

The more intuitives learn to read these energetic impressions, the more accurate their assessments become. Understanding subtle energies and impressions while learning to embrace inspired thoughts can help you create more enjoyable life experiences.

Aura

One very basic concept is that everything is energy, including us. Our body has energy centers called chakras and is surrounded by a multi-layered energy field called auras. According to energy healer

Donna Eden, your aura acts as a protective field buffering you from the physical, emotional, and psychic energies of the environment. Eden states:

> Your aura sends signals into your environment that communicate information about you that attracts specific types of energy to you. The aura holds a set of interrelated fields that are the blueprints for your physical body, your emotions, your awareness, your relationships, and your development.[6]

Eden goes on to say that the aura is often seen as having multiple layers, colors, and shapes that continuously change due to our physical health, emotions, activities, and our environment.[7] The stronger your aura, the healthier you are.

It is also not out of the realm of possibility that a skilled intuitive, such as myself, can recognize disturbances in an aura before they manifest in the body, allowing for accurate predictions and early intervention. Every intuitive interprets aura differently. If I sense a density or darkened area in the liver on my client during a medical intuitive reading or reiki session, the aura will have a particular dark and dense characteristic that is usually associated with anger or fear. I would suggest to the client to have it evaluated by their healthcare provider, as the area could be suspicious. One time, I saw a shredding in the right shoulder muscle in my friend's aura, not in the body, so I told her that she needed to be careful to strengthen that shoulder and avoid heavy lifting. My friend didn't have any issue with the shoulder but would heed the message. A year later,

---

6 Donna Eden, "The Human Aura," accessed May 26, 2020, https://www.innersource.net/em/66-handout-bank1/hbbasicprinciples/199-donna-eden-a-david-feinstein-v15-199.html.

7 Ibid.

she told me that she tore her rotator cuff lifting something very light, but she had done a lot of lifting over the past year.

Our aura is kind of like our own personal bodyguard that can buffer out anything stressful, disturbing, or potentially draining that we come in contact with. There are many ways to strengthen this energy field, which are similar to all the things your doctors have been telling you to do for years to stay healthy: Eat a balanced diet, avoid excessive sugars and fats, get six to eight hours of sleep, exercise thirty minutes a day, avoid illicit drugs or excessive alcohol, avoid extremes in stress, or find balance with emotional situations. Drinking sixty-four ounces or more of water a day will help flush out stagnant energy or negativity that we store in our cellular memory. When you start to feel drained, fatigued, unwell, or disconnected from self, you should have a set of tools to fall back on.

According to *The Crystal Bible*, crystal healing is believed to be effective in strengthening your aura. It is believed that holding, wearing, or having crystals around your physical body can help strengthen and protect you. Labradorite is thought to heal tears within the aura. Amber strengthens the aura, kunzite is used to detach unpleasant thoughts, and black tourmaline deflects radiation and transmutes negative energy. Smoky quartz protects from stressors, negative energies, and absorbs sadness. Amethyst will increase spirituality, watermelon tourmaline increases self-love, and hematite helps to ground and protect. Clear quartz can be energizing, but it amplifies what is already there, so be cautious if you are in a negative space as the crystal will amplify that as well.[8] I do not recommend clear quartz for children. Children tend to do well with amber, citrine, selenite, black tourmaline, but always use your discretion and see how the child responds.

---

8 Judy Hall, *The Crystal Bible* (Cincinnati: Walking Stick Press, 2003), 52, 54, 140, 163, 170, 225, 240, 298, 302.

If you are interested in crystal healing, consider doing some research about which crystals align with what you need. You can buy them at metaphysical shops or stores online. You can also purchase books on crystals to learn more about ways to work with them. I enjoy wearing them as jewelry, placing them around my home, and holding them when I mediate. Try wearing different crystals and write your experiences in your journal. Make note of any changes in how you feel.

Chakras

Just as our aura contains our vital information, our chakras provide a deeper understanding of our physical and emotional well-being. According to Eden in her book, *Energy Medicine: Balancing Your Body's Energies for Optimal Health, Joy, and Vitality*, the chakras (ancient Sanskrit) are "energy stations" on the body that are invisible to the naked eye.[9] The theory of chakras dates back to early Hinduism traditions in India. "Each chakra influences the organs, muscles, ligaments, veins and all other body parts within its energy field."[10] With chakras, not only can you see issues similar to that of the aura, but you can also feel the energy changes. Intuitives often work with the seven most common chakras. Through alternative energy healing techniques, such as reiki, spiritual healing, or hands-on healing, you can balance and clear blockages from your chakras.

Chakras are usually associated with colors, organs, functions, and both positive and negative qualities. If one of your chakras is out of balance, you can demonstrate the negative qualities and vice versa. The seven chakras are described below according to Eden:[11]

---

9 Donna Eden and David Feinstein, PhD, *Energy Medicine: Balancing Your Body's Energies for Optimal Health, Joy, and Vitality* (New York: The Penguin Group, 1998), 147.

10 Eden, *Energy Medicine*, 153.

11 Ibid., 159–179.

- The *first chakra (root)* is red, and the physical body located at the base of the spine. It is associated with the kidneys, adrenal gland, and colon. Positive qualities: stability, health, patience, etc. Negative qualities: insecurity, violence, survival concerns, and survival mode.

- The *second chakra (sacral)* is orange, and the emotional body is located just above the pelvic region in the lower abdomen associated with the sexual glands, prostate, and spleen. Positive qualities: passion, desire, and harmony. Negative qualities: sexual difficulty, jealousy, and purposelessness.

- The *third chakra (solar plexus)* is yellow, or mental body or will, and is located just below the diaphragm. The pancreas, liver, gallbladder, muscles, and nervous system are tied to this chakra. Positive qualities: self-control and personal power. Negative qualities: anger, fear, and digestive issues.

- The *fourth chakra (heart)* is green and is located at the center of the chest. The heart, arms, legs, lungs, and circulation are affected by this chakra. Positive qualities: compassion, acceptance, and harmony. Negative qualities: repression of love and emotional instability.

- The *fifth chakra (throat)* is blue and is located at the neck. Associated with the thyroid, parathyroid, mouth, and throat. Positive qualities: communication and creative expression. Negative qualities: communication issues and lack of discernment.

- The *sixth chakra (third eye)* is violet and is of insight and intuition. The pituitary, ears, nose, and eyes are connected to the third eye. Positive qualities: insight and intuition. Negative qualities: fear, tension, and headaches.

- The *seventh chakra (crown)* is white and the divine intelligence. The pineal gland and the central nervous system are affected by this chakra. Positive qualities: experiencing oneness with Spirit, inspiration, wisdom, or selfless service. Negative qualities: a lack of inspiration, confusion, senility, or alienation.

With practice, you can notice subtle changes in these energy centers to help yourself and others overcome experiences. For instance, when you feel or sense energy over your root chakra, you would most likely feel a change in the energy such as a cool tingling or warm sensation, or just an increased energy pulling you toward it. Each person interprets what they feel differently. Since the physical root chakra focuses on stability and survival, using what you know about that chakra helps you balance.

Start by becoming self-aware of your positive or negative qualities. For example, one of the negative qualities associated with the seventh chakra (crown) is a lack of inspiration. If you find that you are in a creative rut with a chapter in the book you've been working on, tap into the positive qualities of the crown chakra. Find inspiration elsewhere, in nature, in art, in movement.

If you know the polar opposites of the positive and negative qualities of each chakra, you can use them to your advantage to help shift your perspective back to the positive. You can also wear clothes and eat foods that are the color of the chakra as another way to help balance. When I need to give a speech, I tend to wear blue to assist with good communication.

Eating fruits and vegetables packed full of that beautiful green chlorophyll brings vibration to your heart-energy chakra, which is the vital power center for empaths. Eating healthy also supports your immune system as well as your overall energy. Processed foods and foods high in sugar and fat content are a typical part of the American diet, but limiting these types of foods can improve your overall auric strength and vitality. Try making dietary changes for one to three months to see the full benefits. Please be sure to ask your healthcare provider before making any dietary changes.

Essential oils and flower essences are very powerful natural remedies that can assist your chakra and your aura. A few drops of vetiver essential oil applied to your belly button at night is thought to help you feel grounded.[12] It can also help you from taking on other people's energy or emotions. Essential oils can help bring your body's natural energy centers, or chakras, into alignment. Lavender is a fantastic oil to help children reduce stress and stimulation.[13] You can purchase many lavender-scented bath washes and air fresheners, or you can diffuse the oils. Yarrow flower essence is thought to help with "repair[ing] breaks in the aura, close the top of an open aura, and bring[ing] the aura down to the ground."[14] There are hundreds of oils and essence to choose from. Always follow the instructions and ask your healthcare provider.

Being highly sensitive to energies can easily throw your chakras out of balance. Learning to embrace these sensitivities and become familiar with ways to rebalance can empower you to bob and weave around challenges in life instead of feeling overwhelmed. Empaths are highly attuned to people and their environment, and they tend to not have clear boundaries and take on other people's energies. The environmental extremes are very difficult to navigate. If exposed to excessive talking, smells, or noise repeatedly, your nerves can unravel. I struggle with excessive noise when I am trying to concentrate and easily become agitated.

---

12 Connie and Alan Higley, *Reference Guide for Essential Oils* (Spanish Fork: Abundant Health, 2018), 116.

13 Ibid., 78.

14 Trish Mooney, "Subtle Body Sensing: The Impact of Flower Essences In the Human Aura," accessed June 7, 2020, http://flowersociety.org/subtle-body-sensing.htm.

Large crowds and harsh environments such as loud events, violence, or arguing can be very overwhelming. On the other end, empaths will typically thrive in a calm and peaceful environment. That is why most empaths are introverts. Introverts need alone time to recharge their batteries. They often enjoy being in nature, as it is calming to their energy. Empaths tend to be very caring and giving with hearts of gold who try to relieve the suffering of others. Empaths with poor personal boundaries can take on the energies of others and feel physically drained or exhausted, which affects all aspects of their lives.[15] The opposite is also true: an empath with healthy energetic boundaries has the ability to shift the entire energy in a room, enhance harmony in a group, and soothe someone in distress.

Regardless of how you experience this world, the first step to having your chakras in balance is to identify your qualities. If you are experiencing the positive or negative qualities of the chakras, pay attention over the next week and see if you can feel or sense your chakras or aura. What images or colors come into your awareness? It is quite fascinating to pick yourself apart to gain a better understanding of how you work. Remember, we are all learning about ourselves every day and in every situation. The key is to begin to go deeper into the how and whys.

Earthing

Earthing (also known as grounding) refers to being in direct contact with the earth, which causes a *grounding* or calming effect to the body. "The earth has a mild negative charge to it. Over time, especially in modern life, our bodies build up a positive charge.

---

15 Orloff, "The Top 10 Traits of an Empath."

Direct contact with the earth can even out this positive charge and return the body to a neutral state."[16]

To practice earthing, you must be in direct contact with the earth. This can be sitting, walking, or lying on the ground. Have you ever noticed that you sleep better on vacation camping in the woods? That's because being around nature and the trees ground the body and remove excess positive electrons. Our subtle energy bodies need the same kind of grounding to be in balance. Being exposed to electronics like computers, phones, and televisions increases our exposure to electromagnetic frequency (EMF) waves, which cause increased damage from free radicals from the positive electrons. Grounding to the earth balances our energies. This is why many empaths will find nature regenerative.

*Reducing electromagnetic frequency (EMF) exposure is es-*sential in today's society. You can reduce EMFs by unplugging all electronics unless you are using them. In our plugged-in society, we use cell phones and computers all day long. It is recommended that you keep phones and all electronics as far as you can from your physical body for as long as possible. I tell all of my patients to keep their phones off their body. According to a 2013 study, four women under the age forty were diagnosed with breast cancer after having placed their cell phones in their bras for up to ten hours a day for several years.[17] I also ask my patients to keep their phones across the room when they are sleeping to reduce the exposure.

There is growing scientific research about the benefits of earthing, such as an improvement with "inflammation, cardiovas-

---

16 Katie Wells, "Earthing & Grounding: Legit or Hype? (How to & When Not To)," last modified July 30, 2019, https://wellnessmama.com/5600/earthing-grounding/.

17 John West et al., "Multifocal Breast Cancer in Young Women with Prolonged Contact between Their Breasts and Their Cellular Phones," *Case Reports in Medicine*, September 18, 2013, doi: 10.1155/2013/354682.

cular disease, muscle damage, chronic pain, and mood."[18] When I spend time outside, I feel I breathe deeper and I'm better able to relax. Our subtle bodies respond nicely to nature, and it is vital that everyone find balance with nature, especially in this technological age where we all work with electronics. Have you ever noticed that children who play outside more are calmer and have fewer issues with staying focused? How do you feel when you are in nature?

Soaking up the sunlight for only ten minutes a day increases your vitamin D absorption. The sun also helps your body absorb calcium. Sunlight is thought to increase the brain's release of serotonin, which is a hormone that helps you feel focused and more centered. We are all dependent on the use of the sun's energy. The plants take the energy of the sun and store it, then humans take that food and use it for energy.

One of the easiest and cheapest ways to remove toxins, reduce electromagnetic frequency exposure, and feel rejuvenated is taking a sea salt bath. The salt in this process helps to remove the toxins and negative ions. I prefer the natural salts, such as Celtic or Himalayan, but any salt will do. For adults, add one cup of sea salt to your bath as hot as you like and soak for twenty to thirty minutes. For children over five, sprinkle a small amount of salt and soak for no more than ten minutes. Adults can also add one cup of organic baking soda or essential oils. Stir the salt at the bottom, but be sure to set your intention of cleansing all negative or disharmonious energies and rinse off after your soak.

Exercise

The goal of this exercise is to familiarize yourself with the process of earthing. I want you to be more aware of your surroundings and

---

18 Eleesha Lockett, "Grounding: Exploring Earthing Science and the Benefits Behind It," August 30, 2019, https://www.healthline.com/health/grounding.

of any changes in your mood, your body, your energy, and/or your mind after you have gone outside and practiced grounding to the earth. It is recommended to journal your experiences.

- Find a quiet place outside and take off your shoes. You need to be barefoot for this exercise.

- Take note of how you feel and what is going through your mind. Are you anxious, overthinking, relaxed?

- Walk around in your bare feet in the grass or in the sand. If this isn't an option, sit beneath a tree with your back pressed against the bark. The goal is for your body to be touching the earth.

- Take a few deep breaths and try to clear your mind. Notice how your body is feeling as you walk. Is it tense, tight, relaxed? Did you notice a calming of the mind? A change in breathing? A change in your mood? A change in your outlook?

_____

_____

_____

_____

_____

_____

_____

_____

_____

_____

Exercise

Use this meditation anytime you feel the need to strengthen your aura. Before you start, ask Spirit to be with you as protection while you perform this meditation. It is always nice to have the assistance of your spiritual team.

Meditation takes practice, so don't get too caught up in the details if it's not going the way you'd like. The best thing you can do is to carve a little time out each day to practice your meditation.

- Sit in a comfortable position, relaxing your arms with hands gently on your lap.

- Imagine your aura all around you as though you're standing in the middle of a ball of white light. Imagine your crown opening to the divine and the soles of your feet opening and connecting you to the core of Mother Earth.

- Take a few deep breaths. With every inhale, breathe in the beautiful white light of the divine from your crown and into your body. As you exhale, push all the negative energy out of the soles of your feet to Mother Earth.

- When your entire aura and body are filled with the beautiful white light of the divine, imagine expanding your aura out from the side of your body with each breath.

- Push your aura as if you are filling a giant bubble of white light, and envision it expanding, just growing and growing to the size of your house, then your state, then the size of your country, the Earth, the moon . . . just feel the energy change and be present.

- Take notice of how you are feeling and what you are aware of.

- After a few minutes, reverse the process and pull your aura in closer to you with each breath until it is back to normal.

Pull it in, just as you pushed it out . . . back to the size of the Earth, to the size of your country, to the size of your state, your building/house, your room . . . and finally beside your body.

• Be still and take a few breaths, bringing that beautiful white light from your crown straight into Mother Earth, grounding your energy.

How did you feel before and after this meditation? Did you notice any change in your energy level? Any change in your well-being? Did you see colors or have any other sensations occur during the meditation? Write it down in your journal or the space below.

_____

_____

_____

_____

_____

_____

_____

_____

_____

_____

_____

_____

_____

_____

CHAPTER 3

PSYCHIC ABILITIES

What does it mean to be psychic? I am asked that question a lot because people want to better understand how psychics see and interact with the world. To answer this question, we must first understand that we are all born with the same psychic abilities. This chapter will discuss four of the most common psychic abilities: *clairsentience*, *claircognizance*, *clairaudience*, and *clairvoyance*.

We are all born with natural intuitive abilities and psychic tendencies; it is just whether we choose to develop them or not. We can develop them to assist us in navigating the world easier. Some of us are meant to develop our psychic abilities as a profession in this incarnation and some are not, which is perfectly okay as our differences are what makes being human so wonderful. Regardless of our profession, Spirit will always work with us to become the best version of us.

The Four "Clairs"

Clairsentience is to clearly sense or feel "the present, past or future physical and emotional states of others without the use of the normal five senses."[19] It is an extremely heightened form of empathy. It

---

19 "clairsentience," Psychic Library, accessed June 6, 2020, https://psychiclibrary.com/clairsentience/

can be activated without conscious awareness. Many who have this ability are able to use clairsentience without even realizing what is happening. We can manifest this in several different ways: through our instincts and intuition, our empathy and sympathy, and our emotions and physical sensations. When your intuition is sensing, you can have a sudden strong insight or inspiration that seems to appear from out of nowhere.

For example, one day I was at the nurses' station when I saw a patient sitting in the hallway. A strong feeling washed over me, and my heart was beating irregularly and rapidly. I went over to this patient and felt his pulse—it was beating irregularly, which was abnormal and new for him. I immediately ordered that he get an electrocardiogram, which showed an irregular heart rhythm called atrial fibrillation. The patient was then able to get the help that he needed.

When you are empathic, you can literally feel in your body what someone or something else is feeling. If someone is upset, an empath will take that on and also feel upset. I felt this patient's heart rhythm was off before I even took his pulse. After addressing the change in my physical sensation, which I identified as the patient's, the sensation in my body stopped. This is how Spirit can use your physical body as the tool to deliver psychic information. Empaths can sometimes find it difficult to determine the cause of their physical sensations, especially if the sensations are intense. Maybe someone who isn't familiar with their clairsentience might have thought they were having an issue with their own heart. In time, working with Spirit can help you navigate your clairsentience easier. Another example of being clairsentient is when a husband experiences "sympathy pains" when his wife is in labor.

One of the most fascinating ways one can use clairsentience is through emotional attachment. An emotional attachment is a deep, energetic link where you can feel someone else from a distance. I recall experiencing clairsentience many times with Dave, a man I loved very much for many years. I would know when he was thinking of me, and I would instantly feel his energy no matter what I was doing. When I would think of him, he would text, email, or call me that same day. On the day of my induction into the Sigma Theta Tau International Honor Society of Nursing, my teenage son placed his hand on my left shoulder and told me he was so proud of me, but I also felt David standing there with us. Later, my son confessed that he had no idea why he felt compelled to place his hand on my shoulder. When I spoke with David a few days later, he told me that he'd placed his hand on his own shoulder at the time of the ceremony to let me know he was there supporting me and how proud he was of me.

I think it is amazing to be able to physically feel another and to have that be validated. Whenever I'm tuned in to my clairsentience, I can feel pressure, tingling, a cold sensation, pain, and love, to name a few. I use clairsentience in my healing work as a medical intuitive to hone in on areas out of alignment. Sometimes this physical manifestation is to direct your attention toward a certain person. Dave and I would just think of each other and give "energetic hugs," which is when you can feel the person's arms around you. Or I will sense a cold "spot" when Spirit is in the room, or the hairs on the right side of my body always stand up.

Have you ever felt a very strong feeling come over you and you suddenly knew that someone you love was in trouble only to find out later that you were right? Have you ever felt the hairs stand up on the back of your neck or felt like someone was "tapping" on your shoulder? Think about ways in which you have intuitively felt someone else's feelings or felt Spirit. What visceral sensations came over your body? Have you ever felt someone else's feelings so intensely like they were your own?

Psychic abilities are like the muscles of the body, and you need to condition them to work the way you want. The old adage that practice makes perfect comes to mind. You can practice simple exercises to improve your ability to sense Spirit. Throughout this book, I provide easy tips on how to develop your psychic abilities.

A good way to strengthen your "feels" is through a practice of *psychometry*, or sensing something that is not ordinarily sensible. A psychic is able to pick up impressions, visions, thoughts, or events relating to someone just by holding an object, piece of jewelry, photography, or letter belonging to that person."[20] Psychic energies are in every living being and object, and this is known as a *psychic imprint*. These imprints remain with the objects forever, allowing a person to read and interpret the information through feelings, visions, or knowingness. When I purchased antique chairs for my reading room, I took a picture of the chairs and showed it to a fellow medium who immediately described a man sitting in one of the chairs. The chairs were purchased at an antique store in Atlanta, Georgia, and the spirit who'd owned the chairs was very pleased and smiling with my purchase and intention for use. I can feel his presence from time to time when I am sitting in his chair giving readings.

Psychics are portrayed a variety of ways in film. One of the more common scenes is when a psychic holds a family member's object, such as a ring, and is able to read the owner's energy. A psychic does this because touching the object strengthens the connection. We are all made up of energy, and a psychic can read the energy just like reading an aura. The longer the psychic connects to the energy, the stronger the connection is and the ability to receive more information. When I touch an object, I can receive the owner's traits, such as visualize their physical body,

---

20 Ibid., "psychometry."

feel their emotions, the cause of death, or even receive identifying characteristics such as coughing because the owner is a smoker.

There are many situations where psychometry can be very helpful, such as gathering historical information by touching a wall in a building, or obtaining information about a loved one's emotional or physical health by touching a photograph or object. Sometimes a physical location can be revealed in a missing person's case. A lot can be learned about a child who is having problems by touching their toys, which can store information about their emotional state. Have you ever touched something and felt or saw information about its origin? Another time, I was walking through an antique store and came across a beautiful white marble pedestal. I placed my hand on the cold marble and was instantly overcome with a vision of a Catholic church with stained-glass windows. The visual caused me to feel very lightheaded and I thought I was going to pass out. I inquired about the pedestal, and it was confirmed to have been in a church in the early 1900s.

The next time you notice a sensation, make note of it. What were you touching? What were you feeling before you touched the object? What were you feeling as you were touching the object? What knowledge did you gain from touching the object, if any? The more you become hyperaware of these moments, the more you will notice how frequent they become.

Claircognizance is the psychic ability of your inner knowingness or inspired thought. When we receive information, it is perceived through the conscious mind for observation, and then the conscious mind attempts to interpret it. But for a claircognizant, information is not generated by the conscious mind. Typically, the information that comes in or is "downloaded" will have nothing to do with what you were consciously thinking about. Our thoughts are usually ego-based and want to protect us from failure, embarrassment, or disappointment. Information received through claircognizance comes from a place of wisdom from Spirit and often requires you to take a leap of faith.

Early in my career, I knew one of my patients was not telling me what was really going on with his health. I could feel despair and sadness from him, but he denied feeling suicidal or homicidal when asked and said his depression was very mild. He even told me that good things were happening in his life, and that he had a strong support system from his family and his newfound love. But I had a strong suspicion he was not well, so I encouraged him to talk with his mental health counselor and told him to go to the emergency room if he felt suicidal, and he agreed. But something still felt "off," and I wasn't convinced that he was doing well, so I scheduled to see him in two weeks. When his appointment rolled around, he didn't show up. I found out that the night before he had a fight with his girlfriend and committed suicide. One of most challenging things for me is not being able to save someone from themselves. I have had to learn hard lessons over the years that we all have free will to determine our futures, and we all have a unique journey to walk on Earth. All I can do is love, educate, and use my gifts to the best of my ability to help people in the best way that I can.

Have you ever had the sense of knowing someone was not telling the truth despite facts to the contrary? Have you ever had an idea that was truly inspired from out of nowhere? That happens to me a lot. I will receive so many good ideas about all kinds of topics and want to act on them. I recall one occasion where I was questioning Spirit about what I was supposed to be doing next in my life and asked for a clear message. A few days later, I received an offer for a job I hadn't even applied to! Spirit said very clearly in my mind, *It's time to go there*, requiring me to take a leap of faith and move. I was enjoying working as a DNP providing care in a free clinic—a drug and alcohol rehabilitation center and an urgent care center—when the job offer came to join a family practice in another state. This was challenging because I liked where I was working and never thought a move was in order. Thankfully, I took that leap of faith and made the move and was very blessed for having done it.

One thing you may experience with claircognizance is *not* listening but having the hindsight later to say, "I knew it." That recognition is one way to begin to tune in to the subtle delivery of these messages. The other is to act on the information and receive the validation from a positive outcome.

A good example of claircognizance occurs when I am driving. I travel a lot, and in the silence of driving, I experience Spirit very strongly. One afternoon I was getting tired, and I remember *thinking that I should probably pull off at the next exit and get gas*, use the restroom, and get some water. The next stop wasn't for several miles. Being the stubborn person I am, I wanted to keep to a tight schedule, so I pushed on. A few miles ahead, traffic was stopped because of an accident. We were sitting in traffic for over an hour. I thought my bladder would burst! I remember thinking, *I wish I had listened to my intuition and stopped at that rest stop!*

We are all human, and sometimes we are slow learners. I didn't make that mistake again. The next time I took a trip—and every trip thereafter—I make sure to listen to my mind and body. Learning to trust this information when it is coming in allows you to act sooner rather than later. Learning to develop this muscle is asking Spirit to assist you.

Clairaudience is the ability to clearly hear the Spirit in the physical and non-physical worlds. It is a subtle inner voice that offers you warnings or guidance in your inner ear. The best way I can explain clairaudience is to compare it to the voice in your head when you're reading silently but it is a distinctly different voice than your own. This is most often heard from within, but

Spirit has been known to speak outside of you in cases of imminent danger and when Spirit needs to get your attention.

One time, I was driving on the highway when I felt Spirit sitting in the passenger seat and heard a voice that said out loud, "Look out!" Just then, a car pulled over and I swerved out of the way within a split second of being hit. Another time while talking to a patient about why she had made the appointment, I heard a voice internally say, *She is not telling you the truth*, which was easily validated when the patient was caught in a lie. The patient said she was having back pain and was clearly seeking pain medication. She lied about the length, duration, and even the location of the pain then demanded pain medication.

If you haven't heard Spirit, how do you know if you are clairaudient? Some of us are predisposed toward this psychic ability. People who have heightened sensitivities, who hear more than most, or are bothered by loud noises or environments, are usually clairaudient. Musicians often hear the beats or melody internally first.

Have you ever heard Spirit in your head? Perhaps Spirit said something like, "Don't do that," or, "Look out." Have you heard your name when no one was around? Do you need quiet time to gather your thoughts? Does a loud TV or noisy room leave you feeling tired, irritable, or give you a headache? Do you carry on conversations with yourself in your head? Are you hypersensitive to music? Some of us are deeply affected by the vibration of music and can find it challenging to listen to rock music or heavy metal. Many clairaudient people hear ringing or high-pitched sounds in their ears. This can be a great way for Spirit to alert you to paying attention to your thoughts or words. When I experience this type of sound sensitivity, it is usually because my guides are drawing my attention to someone or something. When I acknowledge the ringing and where it's drawing my attention, the ringing will stop. Spirit will sometimes use your stronger muscles to get your attention.

Clairvoyance is the ability to "clearly see" the Spirit through your third eye, your mind's eye. Clairvoyance is the one most people imagine when they think of being psychic. Clairvoyants can see energy fields, auras, Spirit, symbols, colors, numbers, and receive premonitions. Clairvoyants can also experience vivid imaging, which can play out like a movie that you can view and interpret. I tend to see the moving picture when I am listening to someone tell me a story; it is like their perception comes to life. Interpreting what you see is the challenge, as sometimes the meaning or significance is not literal but metaphoric in nature. Use your other psychic abilities to assist your discernment of the information you receive.

I am a strong clairvoyant and have seen angels and Spirit in full body standing with me. One time when I was leaving the grocery store, I felt this cold energy pressing up against me. At first it felt like someone was pushing their cart right up against me. When I turned around, a seven-foot-tall angel was standing there in the reflection of the glass. I once again felt the cold hand on my back, but when I turned to catch a glimpse of the angel, she was gone. I love when my spirit helpers makes their presence known and catch me off guard. It is reassuring that our spirit helpers are always with us even when we are doing the most mundane chores.

Have you ever had a vivid dream that later comes true? Have you ever lost your keys but an image of where you left them flashes in your mind? Have you seen an image of a person in your mind's eye only to receive a call or a letter from that person later on? I love these kinds of synchronistic experiences that remind me just how magical the world is around us.

Putting Your Clair to Practice

Whenever we start something new, there is always an element of fear attached to it. Even if it's something we are excited about, there is still a level of fear, though it may be small, subtle, or even in our subconscious mind. For example, even if you are excited about starting a new job, there are many underlying fears. Will you like your new position? Will you like your coworkers? Will you like your boss? But you take the plunge anyway for your own personal reasons. Time will tell whether it was the right choice. The point being is that you *made* a choice, and with that choice, you approached fear whether you were aware of it or not. Congratulations on choosing to explore your psychic abilities and the many ways they can help you live your best life.

When putting your psychic abilities to practice, you will encounter many fears. There are many ways to develop your clairvoyance, or "seeing," but the first thing you'll need to do is to begin to release your fears. I know this is easier said than done. We all have fears, and sometimes our fears can be so debilitating, not just in our everyday lives but also hindering our psychic abilities. Young children (ages two and younger) are thought to be able to see the spirit world easier. Ask any mother and she will tell you that her baby or toddler will often stare off into a corner of the room when "nothing" is there. Children will laugh and interact with "no one." The belief is that babies and toddlers are wide open and see very easily between the physical and spirit worlds. Fear is thought to be a main reason why people shut off the vision and don't want to see Spirit. It could develop from seeing a frightening image, or parents or others who transfer their own fears to a child.

Have no fear (pun intended)! You can release that fear and move forward. Some choose the path of counseling to find the root cause of fear, while others may release through intention and positive affirmations. Ultimately, you will need to forgive yourself and others if involved. This is not an easy task. Getting over fear— whether it's a newfound fear or deep-rooted—takes time and effort. Some people struggle with fear their entire lives. Everyone is different, and what resonates with someone may not resonate with someone else. In my process of dealing with fear, I need to get to the root cause of the fear, which means going back and healing the losses I felt as a child, seeing all the death before it occurred, and the lack of support I felt. Through years of counseling, energy work, meditation, and learning to let go and release the past, I have been able to trust Spirit, my visions, and my path.

Releasing your fear can allow you to have a clear head so you're able to trust your Spirit connection and build your clairvoyance. *One thing that helps me is the power of intention and repetition.* I have many mantras that I say throughout the day depending on what I am doing. Before you can begin tapping into your psychic abilities, you should try to have a "clean slate." What I mean by this is that you should be open and accepting, and release any fears or preconceived notions and ideas. The letting-go process is one that can be difficult, but it is also healing and transformative.

Here is a quick practice to help you release your fears. Sit in a quiet room. Take slow, deep breaths and say one of the following affirmations either out loud or in your head. Repeat the saying ten times or for at least thirty seconds, or do what you feel guided to do.

I am willing to release all fear of seeing Spirit or my future.

I embrace all that is intended for me in my future.

I forgive myself for shutting down my vision and welcome it back with open arms.

I forgive _____ for the negative feedback surrounding my intuitive insights.

I am safe to see Spirit or my future.
I am surrounded in love.
I am calm and supported by Spirit.

You can choose any of these sayings or another positive affirmation that feels right for you. There is no wrong way to do this. You are using the power of intention, so trust your instincts to guide this process. It is important to have a clear intention because we manifest goals by being specific about what we want to experience. Visualization can be a powerful tool in this process. For instance, after you say your intention, visualize yourself holding balloons, and as you say the affirmation, release the balloons as a representation of letting go. There is something very tangible and concrete when we can "see" a visual representation of our fears floating away in the breeze.

Another way to develop your clairvoyance or vision is through working with your mind's eye, the third-eye chakra. The energy center just above and between your physical eyes is known as the third eye. This chakra is what supplies pictures to the brain. We see ourselves, others, and the world around us through this third-eye lens. This is also termed the "seat of our intuition" where we dream, envision, and strategize on what we want to create.[21] We can work on clearing our third-eye chakra through various ways, such as reiki or energy healing.

Another way to clear the third-eye chakra is to sit in a comfortable position, close your eyes, and take slow, deep breaths while focusing on the third-eye space. As you do this, begin to look for an oval shape that may be purple in color, closed, partially closed, or open. Just continue to breathe, focus, and see if any pictures or

---

21 Helena Sain, "A Journey through the Chakras—The Third Eye," May 3, 2018, https://www.samsaramindandbody.com/single-post/2018/05/03/A-Journey -through-the-Chakras---The-Third-Eye.

symbols come to mind. You may see black-and-white images or a movie may appear. Practice for five to ten minutes a day.

Remember that it takes time to open up completely. With any new skill, repetition is a great way to develop your abilities. Journaling your experiences will help solidify the messages and allow you to see and validate that it is not your imagination. You will begin to see the patterns of how Spirit is working with you and how you are responding to that information. Spend time each day recalling all the ways Spirit communicated to you through visions, images, or symbols. I have created a symbol book where I journal the specific ways Spirit and I work together. Every intuitive receives (or sees) and interprets Spirit's symbols differently. For example, I will see balloons and cake to symbolize a celebration or birthday while others will receive an image of a bouquet of flowers. You will find something that works for you, but I would encourage you to keep track of your progress.

The following exercises are aimed to help you get started on the process of tapping in to your psychic abilities. Remember, we are all human, and we are all beginners at some point, so don't get frustrated if you're having trouble strengthening your abilities. As I've mentioned, repetition and practice is key. Just take a deep breath and relax. I guarantee that you'll surprise yourself!

Exercise

Clairsentience

This exercise will help you tap in to your clairsentience abilities. By the end of this exercise, hopefully you will have been able to use your gut instincts to obtain information about a person through a personal item.

- Obtain an object from a friend who is willing to discuss your findings. It should preferably be a personal or favorite object.

- Sit in a quiet place. Close your eyes and take a few deep breaths.

- Rub your hands together briskly for thirty seconds to "heat up" your energy in your hands.

- Hold the object in one hand and focus on the object.

- As you stare at the object, formulate questions about the person it belongs/belonged to:

  - Characteristics: is the person generous, loving, hard-working, honest, etc.?

  - Emotions: is the person happy, sad, joyful, angry, etc.?

  - What does your "gut" tell you about the energy of the object? Is it positive or negative?

- After you have finished studying the object, tell your friend your findings and ask your friend to evaluate the information you received.

As mentioned, the key to anything is practice, so try doing this with different people. Journal your experiences. You will be amazed at how your readings become more accurate over time.

_____

_____

_____

_____

_____

_____

_____

_____

_____

_____

_____

_____

Exercise

Claircognizance

I use automatic writing to fine-tune my claircognizance. This is when you allow Spirit to "download" information through you while your mind is on the side observing. You put your pen to paper, or fingers to the keys, and just allow them to do the work for you. This type of information tends to be of a high vibration and will often comfort you or provide clarity in some way. It takes some practice, but it can be a very successful way to learn to observe Spirit as well as receive the desired answers you seek.

- Find a quiet place where you will not be disturbed. Set one intention, but make sure it is clear and specific. This can be any particular perspective you want from Spirit. Example: "Spirit, should I buy that house even though I may want to move within the next ten years?" "Spirit, what is my next step on my spiritual journey?" You have to be clear and specific, otherwise you won't receive a clear answer.

- Set a timer so there is a clear beginning and end time. It can be five minutes, ten minutes, or whatever works for you.

- Put your pen to paper, or fingers to keys in a Word document, and let the words flow! You are asking Spirit for guidance on your question or intention, and it should feel effortless because Spirit is working for you. Write whatever comes to mind without judgment. Allow the process to flow organically.

_____

_____

_____

_____

_____

_____

_____

_____

_____

_____

Exercise

Clairaudience

One of the most fun ways to develop your clairaudience hearing is with active listening. Clairaudience is all about listening to the far-off sounds of Spirit. By strengthening this muscle, you will begin to hear Spirit more clearly as the subtle voice in your head that is different from your own voice. Any person who suffers from migraines understands hearing hypersensitivities. This is the same heightened sensation you can receive by practicing these exercises.

My favorite way to practice active listening is by listening to music. Classical music is wonderful for this exercise, as it will provide you with multiple instruments to focus on.

- Select a piece of music, preferably with no singing or lyrics, such as classical or instrumental music. It is suggested to find a song or piece of music that is longer than five minutes.

- Find a quiet place to sit where you will not be disturbed. Take a few slow, deep breaths, and listen to the music.

- Choose one instrument, such as the violin, to focus on until you hear that sound above all other sounds. Follow that instrument throughout the song.

- Next, replay the song but focus on a different instrument, such as the flute or the drums. Repeat the steps above.

After you have done this exercise a few times and feel confident, try this exercise in a public space where you'll be surrounded by a lot of sounds. Follow the same steps above for active listening. Journal your experiences.

_____

_____

_____

_____

_____

_____

_____

_____

_____

_____

_____

_____

_____

_____

Exercise

Clairvoyance

One of my favorite exercises is visualization. If you can visualize an object in your mind's eye as clear as you see with your physical eye, it will assist you in seeing details of Spirit. To practice this, use whatever you want as the object. I often use flowers, crystals, or photographs of the things I enjoy.

- Select an object of choice and place it in front of you. Look at it for a while. Study its shape, its texture, its size. Feel it in your hands and hold it in your palm. Do this for at least one minute or for as long as you feel guided.

- Close your eyes and focus on your third eye just above and between your physical eyes and imagine what that object looks like. Try to recall what the object looks like down to the smallest detail. Does it show color first then begin to develop shape? Does the object show up immediately then fade out? Is the object clear or hazy?

- When you can see the object clearly in your mind's eye, select another object and repeat the process.

The more you do this exercise, the easier it will be to recall what the object looks like. Journal your progress. Seeing objects clearly with your mind's eye takes a lot of practice, so do not get discouraged. Have patience and trust the process. It took me years to see Spirit and objects as clear as I see with my physical eyes, and there are times I still struggle with it. This is not about perfection; this is a process that takes time, but you can do it!

CHAPTER 4

SPIRITUAL AWAKENING

O ther than being innately intuitive and being self-aware, some people begin to become aware of their intuition after what is called a *spiritual awakening*. This is when you experience a paradigm shift or initiation into the process of awakening through connecting to your higher self and higher consciousness as you begin on your spiritual path.[22] Once this occurs, you will begin to question and challenge your old thoughts, values, and religious or spiritual beliefs. You begin to see through the lies of the world around you. You start to realize that your connection with your higher self brings genuine fulfillment. Without experiencing a spiritual awakening, we can continue to pursue the pleasures of the world of things, power, and money, but they are never able to provide the same level of fulfillment or lasting joy.

My own spiritual awakening was a slow process that took years of looking at myself to discover what I believed, what I valued, and where I was putting my attention in my life. Then it was very painful to discover that I was believing in things that I no longer felt true. I began to really look at various religions and my Lutheran upbringing. I was searching for a place or a belief system that aligned with my thoughts, feelings, and ideals, a way to nurture

22 Melanie Beckler, "What Is Spiritual Awakening?" accessed June 10, 2020, https://www.ask-angels.com/spiritual-guidance/spiritual-awakening/.

my spiritual development from my mid-thirties to my mid-forties. This led me to study and become an ordained Reverend with the Fellowships of the Spirit in Lily Dale, New York.

That was just one area of my life where I was compelled to look deeper, and the result of my belonging to a spiritual community that helped me grow as a person was a blessing. But it wasn't an easy path. There was a lot of confusion and heartache along the way. How would you feel if you were to question everything about yourself? Who you are, what your values are, and what your purpose is here on Earth? I was questioning if there was a plan before I was born, and if there is reincarnation, and what did all of it mean to my beliefs and views. It was a messy process, but I like messy!

Throughout this spiritual search, I began to question and re-awaken my mediumship and natural intuitive abilities. The more I questioned, the more that came up for me to heal. For example, I had a lot of resentment toward my mother for things that occurred when I was growing up. Through a lot of forgiveness, counseling, and energy work, I began to resolve those feelings to find a place of forgiveness and love. I find it fascinating how complex we are as humans and the depths to which we hold our emotions. That can lead to a lot that may need to be healed. Then I began to question my purpose in this earthly life, and what I was meant to do and how could Spirit help me fulfill this purpose. In those early years, my life perspective shifted from focusing on the self to looking at life through the lens that we are all one, and we are all looking for ways of healing the body, mind, and spirit.

Sometimes there is a catalyst or life-changing experience for a spiritual awakening, such as a near-death experience, a life-threatening illness, a mental breakdown, meeting a soulmate, or a visitation with Spirit that can cause disbelief, shock, and awe. But trust me on this: you will know it when it happens. When you are on the path of a spiritual awakening, it is hard to ignore, and there is no denying it.

Even though I am a natural psychic and was on a spiritual path at a very young age, I was not what I would have called "spiritually awoken" until after a near-death experience. I was thirty-seven at the time, and it was a sunny and humid day. My friend Sabrina and I were washing our motorcycles at the car wash. We were discussing all the activities for the coming day and how excited we were to be a part of a fundraiser that would help mothers with children in need. Over two hundred bikes were part of the fundraiser, and we were traveling several miles.

On the day before the final leg of our travels, I was cleaning the dirt and muck off my bike when I heard a male voice say, *Do not ride.* I stopped and looked up at Sabrina. I must have had a crazy look on my face because she asked me what was wrong. I was nervous, so I blurted, "Listen, I have a really bad feeling about riding tomorrow. I am hearing this voice telling me not to ride."

Sabrina's eyes grew wide. "A voice?" she asked.

"Yeah . . . um . . . it's hard to explain. But a voice is telling me not to ride, and I have a pain in the pit of my stomach."

Sabrina seemed hesitant, but then she chuckled and said, "Oh, don't be silly, Michelle. I'm sure everything will be fine." And we continued to wash our bikes.

I clearly received multiple warnings from Spirit the next day about riding my motorcycle. My clairaudience warnings started the morning off when I clearly heard, *Do not ride today*, and then my motorcycle would not start. Next there were several clairvoyance warnings, as I saw an angel standing in front of my bike shaking her head. But we had already made several stops on our path, and I chose to ignore the messages. So I rode.

As the day went on, I encountered many trials and tribulations. At every stop, my bike had trouble starting. When I was on the road, it felt as though Spirit was gently shaking my bike and making it swerve so I wouldn't gain full speed. I'd finally had enough of the emotional roller coaster of Spirit attempting to stop me from riding. At each stop, Spirit would be communicating with me in some way, warning me of danger and to stay off the bike. Angels were talking to me, but I wasn't acknowledging their warnings. I was clearly not connecting because I didn't realize I was in any real danger since my angels were with me all day. Of course I was wrong.

At the last stop, my angels asked me to not get back on the bike, and an intense sense of dread washed over me. I asked a few of my friends to leave early with me, as I did not want to go alone and just wanted to go home. There were about five of us who left early and headed down the windy mountain. Along the drive, my motorcycle kept pulling me from side to side, and I wasn't fully in control of it. Spirit was now yelling at me to get off the bike as I was driving. I replied, *Just get me home and I will get off.* Suddenly, a vision came to me for a split second and I saw an accident. "Oh shit, I'm going to wreck!" I yelled, and then everything went black.

Bystanders recalled seeing me riding as if nothing was wrong, sitting up straight, and then I went completely limp and wrecked going fifty-five miles per hour. I rolled twenty-five feet until my bike and my body came to a dead stop in the only gravel patch on the curvy mountain road.

At the moment of the accident, still riding, I had blacked out, as if someone pulled me out of my body, and I blinked and woke up in a white room surrounded by familiar energy. I knew these energies to be spiritual beings, guides, ancestors, and healers who all sat around a big table in this white room. The energy was cool and silent in the presence of angels. They all sat at the table with me and went through what was called a "life review." I was able to see a highlight movie reel of my life, the people I have helped, and the things I have said that affected other people in positive and negative ways. I learned there was a life plan I decided on before my birth about the experiences I wanted and why. It was extremely humbling to see the things I have done throughout my life and the ways in which even the tiniest action could profoundly affect others. I was given the option to stay in the spirit world or come back and finish my life and lessons on Earth. To this day, I have not processed everything I experienced in that time on the other side.

That moment on the other side was a *choice point* on my life journey. While in the white room, I clearly remember arguing with Spirit that I could not have chosen this life because it had been very difficult. Spirit explained that I, along with everyone in that room, decided my life plan before I was born. Then I was shown, for the lack of a better word, a scene from my time before I came into this life. I was a pure light body and my angels were sitting in a similar room discussing many aspects of my life on Earth and the things I wanted to learn, to heal, and to grow spiritually. To say the least, I was completely in awe and did not even know how to begin to process that thought. After my discussions with Spirit, I was encouraged to come back and realign with my purpose and life plan. Again, this was my experience, and I am aware that it may not align with your own beliefs.

Afterward, I was instantly back in my body with friends attempting to help me. I remember thinking, *Oh my God, I'm alive*, and jumped to my feet to the shock of everyone who had gathered. It took several years to integrate all that I experienced physically, mentally, and spiritually. That everything I experienced—positive and negative—was all planned to help me grow spiritually. This began my spiritual awakening and my understanding of life and the afterlife with a new perspective. At that point in my life, I was spiritual and believed in my experiences with God and Spirit, but I would not say I followed one religion. Since that day, I have been aware of how Spirit has been interacting with me daily in all aspects of my life.

Another way you can have a spiritual awakening is when there is a shift in perspective from events such as a move, relationship issues, and needing a change. Maybe your lifestyle is suffering because you're working too much and are not able to spend enough time with your family. Maybe you're depressed and you aren't properly taking care of yourself by eating healthy or exercising. These types of things lead to a discomfort of a lifestyle that's not fitting any longer. A spiritual awakening can occur once you begin a journey of discovery and your field of awareness expands and allows new information to stream in. This is when you can begin to have synchronicities, premonitions, vivid dreams and visions, and improved clairvoyance and clairaudience.

One of the more common ways that people have a spiritual awakening is when they seek to understand their spiritual connection. This is experienced through having a thirst for spiritual knowledge, seeking your true purpose, seeking out like-minded individuals, seeking intuitive readings or classes, or traveling to sacred spaces.

Have you experienced a spiritual awakening? What did that process look like for you? Was it a subtle experience, or did it take moving heaven and earth to awaken your sense? Do you know someone who has had these kinds of experiences? If so, what did it look like?

As you move through a similar process of self-discovery after a spiritual awakening, you may find that the process is easier if you develop your connection with Spirit and your psychic abilities. This can be done with the assistance of many tools such as mediation, Qigong, reiki, to name a few. After time and practice, and trusting your connections, you will discover the ease of following your intuition as it guides your experiences.

Signs of a Spiritual Awakening

Deepak Chopra, a renowned spiritual leader, explains that the process of spiritual awakening happens "when you are no longer living in a dream world where you filter everything through your ego and focusing on the future and the past. Instead, you have an almost simultaneous awareness of your individual self and the connection between that and everything else."[23]

There are many signs of a spiritual awakening, and how they are described depends on the source. I have chosen Chopra's trainings, as they resonate with me the most. The ten most common signs of a spiritual awakening are: observing your patterns (noticing), feeling a sense of connection, letting go of attachment, finding inner peace, increasing your intuition, having synchronicity, increasing your compassion, removing the fear of death, increasing authenticity, and flourishing.[24]

This process typically begins with questioning your personal beliefs and values. Chopra labels this as "noticing." Often we are so busy living life that we are not asking the big questions of why we are behaving in a certain way or why we feel what we feel. Starting to become more self-aware of our actions and thoughts leads to a desire to make change, which is often a lonely contemplation as you let go of the old.

Throughout this transformation, you move into a period of reconnecting with your community and loved ones. Often people find a new sense of responsibility to help improve the world and those they share it with. Once this growth occurs, you tend to want to let go of items you no longer use, and you want to have more

---

23 Tamara Lechner, "10 Common Signs of Spiritual Awakening," February 13, 2019, https://chopra.com/articles/10-common-signs-of-a-spiritual-awakening.
24 Ibid.

freedom and less belongings. Letting go of old beliefs or behaviors that are not helpful can help you grow.

Next you'll want to find inner peace. The Dalai Lama describes inner peace like stubbing his toe—he still experiences an emotional charge, but it is fleeting."[25] I feel inner peace during and after meditation, and then once I begin my day, that feeling of peace can fade.

Some of these phases will overlap as you move through them. Often you will find a time of increased psychic abilities and intuition as you declutter your mind and life. You may become more aware of the magic of synchronistic events as if the universe is conspiring to make magic happen. I have found my own life to be filled with such events, and learning to trust them was a challenge early on, but I have been very grateful they have led me right where I need to be.

One such instance changed my life for the better. Several years ago, I was attending a five-day workshop on acupressure. During the lunchbreak with a friend, I had a vision of a woman with long brown hair sitting on a stump in the middle of the forest. The woman stood up and beckoned me to follow her down a wooded path that opened up to rows of small cottages. She went into one of the cottages and waved for me to follow her.

When I explained what I'd seen to my friend, her eyes widened. "I know exactly where that is! It's Lily Dale, New York," she exclaimed. "You must go right away and have a reading by one of the best mediums, Elaine Thomas."

Lily Dale, New York is the oldest and largest Spiritualist camp in the world. It is a very magical place where mediums live and travel for like-minded community events, educational workshops, and church services. Just outside of their gates is Fellowships of the

---

25 Ibid.

Spirit Lakeside School of Spiritual Healing and Prophecy, which is where I studied and became an ordained Reverend.

My friend insisted we look up Lily Dale immediately after lunch. It just so happened that the esteemed Reverend Elaine Thomas, the longest standing registered medium in Lily Dale and the co-founder of Fellowships of the Spirit, was teaching a spiritual insight development course in three weeks. I immediately signed up without reading about the course or looking much into Lily Dale. That was very unusual for me, as I typically looked into a place I planned to go, did a lot of research on the area, on places to stay, eat, and so on. But I just trusted Spirit on this. When I asked Spirit if I should go, I received a clear *yes*. Spirit also told me that I should stay at the Jewel, which was a beautiful, quaint guest cottage, so I booked it.

On the first night of the class, I was so excited I sat in the front seat. Reverend Elaine Thomas asked if she could give me a reading. Of course I said yes! Elaine went on to describe Bernie, a woman who was like a mother to me. She described Bernie's fun sense of humor, her unique sarcastic wit, and her beautiful way of looking at life. But when Elaine said, "You move through the light in a blink," my jaw dropped. Bernie and I would discuss many topics regarding death and psychic abilities while sitting on her back porch. One day, when I was around ten years old, I had asked her what the death process really felt like. Bernie answered, "I bet you move through it in a blink."

Tears flowed down my cheeks after Elaine said that about Bernie, and I knew without a doubt that Bernie was standing right beside me. That moment changed my life, and I knew I was in the right place to reconnect with Spirit, my mediumship, and my loved ones on the other side. I was overcome with such love and joy from the environment. I felt a strong sense of connection to the place. I knew I had been there before, and it felt like coming home. At the time of this writing, I continue to visit Lily Dale yearly and connect with friends and learn through workshops.

As I gained a deeper understanding, I was able to accept death as a natural part of life. This was made easier for me because of my faith. Once I began to open back up to the communication with loved ones who'd passed into the spirit world, and through my work assisting others with their communication with their loved ones, I was able to accept this step of the process much easier. My work helps me trust that there is not death but a shift from one world to another.

As you move along your spiritual awakening path, you will find a phase of increased compassion and empathy. You may feel more action-oriented to help improve the earth. As you spend more time in a peaceful state, you are closer to becoming more of your authentic self and living your truth. For many, this can be difficult to navigate. The key to shifting my perspective is through meditation, self-awareness of self-talk and identifying, stopping old programming tapes in my intuitive mind, and going deep within to process and heal aspects of self. After all these years, I have finally reached a place of overall well-being. Everyone is different; you may go through these stages in a different order and at a different point in your life.

Physical Symptoms

There are some physical symptoms associated with the spiritual awakening process, though this does differ for everyone. I have experienced several symptoms, sometimes a few at a time. After my motorcycle accident, I began to see, feel, hear, and smell Spirit again, which is known as "amplifying the senses." Some people become very sensitive to the environment, which can show up as seasonal allergies, food allergies, or intolerance for certain foods such as animal protein. I have witnessed many intuitives whose bodies have become more sensitive to processed foods, processed meats, and often develop stomach and digestive issues. Some in the New Age movement might say that your body's energy frequency is changing and requires a cleaner diet of fruits, vegetables, and unprocessed foods. I personally have found this to be the case when I eat beef. I get abdominal pain and cramps after eating beef, but that never bothered me before my accident.

Some people also develop issues with sleep. I had terrible insomnia during my spiritual awakening. I was only sleeping one to four hours a night for many years, and when I did sleep, the dreams were so vivid and intense it was difficult to make sense of them. I felt dizzy or lightheaded most days. This is thought to be from *adjusting to a new vibration of energies and not being "grounded,"* as New Agers say. Being *grounded* means being "present in your body and connected with the earth. When you're grounded, you allow yourself to feel centered and balanced no matter what's going on around you."[26] Practicing earthing, meditating, and using crystals such as jasper or shungite, helps me to feel grounded. I recall meeting certain individuals and their energy just blowing me over until I learned techniques on how to feel grounded.

Being clairsentient, I am able to feel my own and others auras, and through a lot of practice I can pick up on the smallest of changes. The best way to explain this is when you're running late. You're invited to a party and you are rushing around as you get ready. Then you hit every traffic light. Your energy is scattered, you feel restless, anxious, and just want to get there. At this point, you are not calm, centered, or grounded. When you finally arrive

26 Irene Langeveld, "Why Grounding Can be Difficult Sometimes and What to do About It," last modified February 24, 2020, https://www.mindbodygreen. com/0-17987/why-grounding-is-difficult-for-highly-sensitive-people-what-to-do-about-it.html.

to your destination late, you walk into the room feeling frazzled, and the energies of the room will feel stronger since you are not balanced. You are not able to navigate your sensitivities, and you could easily feel overwhelmed by other people. Whereas if you meditated and gave yourself plenty of time to arrive at your destination, you would feel calm, centered, and grounded. When you enter the room more balanced, you are better able to manage other people's emotions and feelings.

When I was going through my spiritual awakening, I would often experience fluctuations with my immunity, as I would frequently get sick and feel run down, but on the other end, I would also feel energized and healthy. Learning what I was eating and how it was affecting my body was key to balancing my immunity. Of course, if you notice a rapid change in your health during this period, it might be due to the drastic change in your mind-body-soul connection. If no logical everyday reason can be found, such as prior illness, family stress, injury, relationship meltdown, etc., you should see your healthcare provider, but keep in mind that a metaphysical explanation can also be the cause. For instance, feeling a lot of pain in the liver region can represent suppressed anger emotions.

With all the ways you can experience a spiritual awakening, it can be challenging to navigate the physical and emotional symptoms that can arise. Learning to find your center of balance and to quiet the mind has been the key for me to be present in the moment and truly experience everything that crosses my path. Understanding what I need to be able to feel centered, balanced, and recharged develops over time, and it's different for everyone. We must begin to let go of the expectations of others and to truly listen to what our bodies, minds, and souls are trying to tell us so that we can live with more ease and grace. Becoming more self-aware will allow us to intuitively sense when we are in balance and when we need adjustments.

Exercise

The purpose of this exercise is to notice areas of your life where you are not in a place of well-being and begin to allow yourself the freedom to explore what that means for you. Becoming more self-aware of your feelings regarding all areas of your life allows you to prioritize where you want to improve.

- Sit in a quiet place with your journal.

- Think about the areas of your life that you are working on autopilot and/or giving minimal effort (e.g., your relationships, work, spiritual growth, diet, health, etc.). Write down what comes to mind. Remember, there is no judgment—just observe where your mind takes you.

- Choose one area to focus on.

- Create two columns: "positive" and "negative."

- Think about your feelings—positive and negative—associated with that area (e.g., where are things going right, what needs improvement, what you desire to change, etc.) and write them down in the appropriate column.

Now that you have created a list of positives and negatives on an aspect of your life that needs clarity, you can begin to move in a direction where you feel peace and well-being. Practice this exercise with one topic at a time and for as long as you need until you can find a happier space to live within this area of your life.

CHAPTER 5

SELF-AWARENESS

A friend of mine and I were at an ice cream shop sitting at the table in the back near the window. She was talking about how upset and stressed she was at her job. "I always end up at this ice cream shop when I'm upset. I don't know why, but I find it so comforting to eat ice cream. But I always pay for it later with a lot of stomach pains and gas," she said.

I found her statements to be so powerful in how it was directing her behavior. So we changed the topic to look at her emotional eating despite the negative effect of eating the ice cream. It was like the proverbial light bulb went off. She had a self-awareness moment where she remembered sitting with her mother and eating ice cream after any emotionally upsetting event occurred. She realized she found comfort in sitting with her mother for guidance and support, not the actual ice cream. Once her mother passed into the spirit world, she began to invite a friend to do the same activity to provide the love and support. She never realized she was developing an unhealthy relationship with food over her emotions. She also realized she was lactose intolerant and does not eat ice cream to this day.

What is self-awareness? The saying, "know thyself," was inscribed on the temples in Kemet and Luxor of ancient Egypt. Socrates, who taught that unexamined life is not worth living, said: "To know thyself is the beginning of wisdom." The *Merriam-*

Webster Dictionary defines *self-awareness* as "an awareness of one's own personality or individuality."[27] I see self-awareness as be-coming aware of every aspect of the body-mind-spirit con-nection that makes up your unique energetic signature. This includes knowledge of your thoughts, actions, and feelings, how you monitor and manage your internal and external worlds, and how they are all connected. We are very powerful beings, and our minds are skillful at storing information. Through our life experiences, we all too often become emotionally conditioned to react in a particular way when we encounter a similar event in the future. Through self-awareness, we can become conscious of these conditioned patterns of behaviors, or "old tapes," as I like to call them, and act consciously rather than react passively.

Research in the field of self-awareness demonstrates our ability to monitor our thoughts, behaviors, and emotions, which is vital to understanding ourselves. People who are self-aware tend to have a positive outlook, are compassionate, and usually follow through with a goal or action. In 2010, Green Peak Partners and Cornell's School of Industrial and Labor Relations conducted a study of "72 executives at public and private companies with revenues from $50 million to $5 billion," and it was found that "a high self-awareness score was the strongest predictor of overall success."[28]

If becoming self-aware is so important, why isn't everyone working on self-awareness? I believe it's a combination of things that make this process difficult. We tend to operate on autopilot and consciously check out and stop paying attention to what is happening in and around us. With our busy lifestyles, it can be

---

27 *Merriam-Webster. Dictionary*, s.v. "self-awareness," accessed June 9, 2020, https://www.merriam-webster.com/dictionary/self-awareness.

28 Victor Lipman, "All Successful Leaders Need This Quality: Self-Aware-ness," *Forbes*, November 18, 2013, https://www.forbes.com/sites/victorlipman/2013/11/18/all-successful-leaders-need-this-quality-self-awareness/#d9b9c701f068.

difficult to stop and smell the roses when there is a huge list of responsibilities or family matters requiring our attention. Or perhaps we consciously decide to avoid looking at ourselves in the mirror to address the underlying issues. It can be upsetting to *really* look at ourselves, to see our less than flattering responses or actions, or in some cases, experiences that are too painful for an empath. For example, let's say you had your heart broken when a relationship abruptly ended. Instead of focusing on the blessings for personal growth or lessons the relationship was meant to address, you focus on the pain of loss. You're overwhelmed with heartache that you're not able to see old patterns of behavior or how the relationship was not meeting your needs. In these instances, we tend to see things through rose-colored glasses and distort the issues. The old saying that "time heals all things" rings true. Time usually allows us to see things in a more accurate light and for us to heal and let go.

To make changes in our behaviors, it takes time and staying conscious in the present moment with lots of repetition. According to a study on how habits are formed by Philippa Lally, a health psychology researcher at the University College London, it can take 18 to 254 days for a new behavior to become automatic. "On average, it takes more than 2 months before a new behavior becomes automatic—66 days to be exact."[29] Have you tried to change a behavior and ever noticed resistance? In the case of my friend and her relationship with ice cream, she had to change her lifestyle in order to stop her emotional eating. The benefit was that she lost weight, felt better, and learned to develop a healthier coping method for stress.

Are you self-aware? Do you truly know who you are? The saying "stay true to yourself" is popular on social media, but how

---

29 James Clear, "How Long Does it Actually Take to Form a New Habit? (Backed by Science)," accessed June 9, 2020, https://jamesclear.com/new-habit.

do you do this if you are not aware of who you are at a soul level? There are several ways we can work on uncovering the vast aspects of ourselves. Understanding your story and discovering your True North is a powerful place to start. According to Bill George, a professor at Harvard Business School and author of *True North: Discover Your Authentic Leadership*, your *True North* is your internal compass that is developed from your beliefs, values, and the principles of who you are at the deepest level. George says that you have to know your authentic purpose first, what is important to you, and what you value in order to make purposeful and mindful choices to get where you want in life.[30] Only then can you define your legacy.

I remember an activity in college where we wrote our obituary or the legacy we would leave. The way people chose to frame their stories was fascinating. It revealed what they valued most, whether it was a successful career, a loving family, the people or experiences that had the most impact, and their passions and lessons. My obituary read a little something like this:

Michelle Walker. 77. Dies at home with family of natural causes. A doctor and medical intuitive treating patients holistically to alleviate suffering in the body, mind, and spirit. She was instrumental in developing protocols that integrated Eastern and Western medicine to cure disease in the body. She was known for her compassionate touch, sense of humor, generous nature, and tenacious will to push through any circumstance. She attributed to her connection with Spirit for her strong guided leadership in all areas of her life. She was preceded in death by her husband, survived by her son and daughter, and

---

30 Bill George, "True North: Discover Your Authentic Leadership," March 28, 2007, https://www.billgeorge.org/articles/true-north-discover-your-authentic-leadership/.

four grandchildren. In lieu of flowers, please make a donation to one of her favorite charities, the Humane Society and the Boys and Girls Club of America.

I learned a lot about myself and what I wanted and had not yet achieved. I had to think about what legacy I could leave behind to help others. I thought about how I was living my life and what would people say about me if they had to write my obituary tomorrow, and if I would like what was said. It was a self-awareness lesson I will never forget. I highly recommend trying it for yourself.

How can you find your authentic self, your True North? Look around your home or office and take note of what you have placed to fill in those spaces that represent what you value. Identify the *objects that mean the most to you and think about how they* demonstrate your values. This may include items of your interest, inspiration, or hobbies, photos of family and friends, or perhaps artwork. What do you surround yourself with? What do the things you see reveal about you? What did you learn that you didn't realize about yourself?

How you spend your time reflects your higher values. People will always make time for what they feel or value as a priority. Years ago, while in the process of quitting smoking, a light bulb went off in my head about how much time in my day revolved around a cigarette. It was a truly mind-blowing revelation that strengthened my resolve to quit forever. Time was a priority for me, as I was working full time as a nurse with two jobs, raising a teenage son, and completing my bachelor's degree. When I added up how much time, in minutes, I spent taking a cigarette break, it came out to over an hour each day. That's seven hours a week! That's twenty-eight hours a month!

What would you spend your time on if you didn't have to worry about obstacles such as money, time off from work, etc.? When we do not honor ourselves and place other people's values as the top priority, we can fall into what I call the "mom syndrome." Every mom knows exactly what this feels like; they let themselves be the last priority by incorporating their significant other, their children, and sometimes their parents and friends' values into their lives. This can leave us unfulfilled, uninspired, and even resentful.

Feeling recharged and energized from doing what you love is the perfect way to use your energy. We often feel tired when we engage in activities we do not value. A perfect example of this is when you are working at a job that you do not enjoy. You are there just to make money to pay the bills versus working on something you are passionate about. To truly embrace ourselves at the deepest level, we need to gain this knowledge and demonstrate courage to change the things we are not in alignment with. When you're doing what you love and loving what you do, you exude vitality.

Money is also energy, and how you spend it reflects what you value most, which most of the time is in conflict with how much you make. I find this to be true and fascinating. Some of my patients tell me that they don't have money for their ten-dollar medication copays but they smoke a pack of cigarettes a day, which costs around seven dollars, and they'll have a six-dollar cup of Starbuck's coffee. It's clear that the priorities are a little conflicted. We all must define what we prioritize in our own lives.

Are you an organized person requiring structure, or do you prefer to live by the seat of your pants? I suspect most of us are a combination of both based on our higher priority at the time. Take notice of your day and see if things are running smoothly or if there is chaos. By noticing which areas are more chaotic you can evaluate their level of priority in your life. Sometimes if there is something we don't want to address and try to ignore, the chaos will force us to address it. An example of this would be if you eat junk food to relieve your feelings of depression. But because you are eating extra calories, you are gaining weight, which contributes to your depression. The cycle will continue until you address the root cause of the issue.

We frequently think about what is most important to us. What occupies your thinking most? When your mind wanders, where does it go, and is there a reoccurring theme? What do you envision for yourself? Energy flows where attention goes. This is how we co-create our reality. What you focus on will allow you to manifest into reality. Perhaps a new relationship, enhanced spiritual abilities, cleaner oceans, or spiritual enlightenment? Words are very powerful and have the ability to build us up or tear us down. Monitoring self-talk is crucial because our internal dialogue is constant. What do you say to yourself—whether it's out loud or in your mind—will have an effect on your mental, physical, and emotional health. The two most powerful words in the English dictionary are *I am*. Anything you say after those words are commands you send into the universe to manifest. Is your self-talk positive or negative? Are there frequent patterns that come up?

I believe inspiration is a key to happiness. We tend to find it easy to discuss the things we are most passionate about and with people who are of like minds. When we are speaking with people whose values clash with our own, it can be challenging to stay engaged. I like to play the game of what I call "I wonder." I allow myself to just think and ask myself questions, which helps me gain a better understanding of myself and how I am interacting in the world. What does the energy of others show you? What can you stay up all night talking about with a dear friend? I can engage with my friends on so many topics that we typically lose track of time. What moments of your life have inspired you? I am inspired by people's life stories. What are your goals, short-term and long-term? Allow your mind to wonder what your life would be like if you already achieved them.

Discovering our strengths and weaknesses can be difficult if we are not completely honest during this process. We need to dig deep and take our time to answer these questions, and then we need to answer them again in six months or a year to reevaluate. I find that my self-assessment changes over time, and it is empowering to see the payoff from the rollercoaster ride of the blessings and struggles. When we understand the way we think, act, react, and experience the world, we are better able to be centered, balanced, and successful in our endeavors. Learning to understand the subtle changes within ourselves allows us to trust the intuitive information we receive while allowing for faster self-correction when we sense we are out of balance. I am successful at remaining present and calm, which allows me to work from a place of love and compassion. I'm aware of how I'm feeling and can analyze what I need to be my best self by using multiple techniques such as body scanning, mindfulness, and meditation.

Self-awareness of the body can assist you on your journey in several ways. As mentioned, when you are in tune with your body, you are in tune with your emotional and spiritual self. *Body scanning* is when you systematically scan through the body with your mind, tuning your awareness to all sensations of your body. It is considered a form of progressive meditation. Body scanning can help you recognize and feel your body sensations and what you are picking up from others around you. It will also reveal to you if there are any areas that can be brought into your conscious awareness emotionally, intellectually, and spiritually. The goal is to notice tension and visualize it releasing out of the body. Our bodies are sensors assisting us to understand what we are experiencing and why. You can do systematic body scans or just one area of the body, but the more you practice the more proficient you will become. It will enhance your ability to bring your full attention to the present moment while allowing you to feel the sensations without trying to change or judge them.

I use this technique daily, and when I notice I am off my normal balance, I will remove myself from the stimuli and redirect my energies. I perform a "quick scan" version of the body-scanning meditation just before I leave my house to assist me in knowing where I am physically and mentally for the day. I also enjoy doing this before I go to work, before I enter a public place, and before parties or events to monitor the change and redirect my energy into alignment. After a few hours or so, or if something emotionally triggering occurs, I "check in" with myself and perform another scan so I am better able to determine how far off my baseline I have become. This also helps me pick up subtle energies from other people, and I can do what I need to do in order to avoid becoming triggered.

Exercise

This is a beginner body scanning exercise. It is designed to help you notice subtle changes within and around you. The idea is to bring awareness to each part of your body and if there is any pain, feeling, or emotion that comes to your awareness as your mind scans. Our bodies hold a lot of emotions and tension, and once we are aware of it, we can acknowledge the discomfort and relax. Keep notes of your progress in your journal or in the space provided on the next page.

- Sit in a quiet space. Close your eyes and take a deep breath as you begin to settle into your physical body. Be present in the moment and allow the energy to flow freely throughout your body.

- Pay attention to the physical feelings in your body: pain, discomfort, coolness, warmth, tension, or tightness. If you notice any discomfort you can make minor adjustments. Make sure that you are comfortable.

• Next, slowly become aware, or scan, your body from the top of your head down to your toes. Begin with your head, then move down the face. Notice your eyes sitting in their sockets. Notice your lips and your tongue in your mouth. Your jaw might be too tight or clenched, so adjust that by opening your mouth slightly or unclenching your teeth.

• Scan your body in this intimate way all the way down to your toes—the neck, anterior chest, posterior chest, abdomen, lower back, hips, right leg, right foot, left leg, left foot . . .

• As you scan your body, notice how good and relaxed you feel.

• Breathe in white light to clear out any areas of the body to make them all feel in balance and alignment again.

• When you are done body scanning, walk around the room. Notice any pain or discomfort.

• Ask Spirit, "Is this pain mine or theirs, and if it is theirs, please take it away." Be open to allow Spirit to release the sensations, and thanking them for the intuitive information will allow you to flow in and out of those sensations.

_____

_____

_____

_____

_____

_____

CHAPTER 6

MINDFULNESS

There is a lot of talk in the New Age spiritual community about "practicing mindfulness," and in this chapter, you will discover what mindfulness is and how you can incorporate it into your life. *Mindfulness* is our ability to be fully present and aware of who and what we are, as well as where and what we're doing. "The goal of mindfulness is to wake up to the inner workings of our mental, emotional, and physical processes."[31] Being centered in the present moment allows us to not overly react or feel overwhelmed by what's going on around us. Our mindfulness is available for us anytime, but we tend not to use it when we are busy and on autopilot. It is easier to use when practiced daily. Learning to tune in to or bring self-awareness to our thoughts and emotions can dramatically improve our quality of life. There is growing research that suggests consistent mental training that occurs with mindful meditation may help keep the brain's mental capacity intact, thus delaying the aging process. In a 2016 study, researchers found that while the brain normally deteriorates as part of the aging process, age-related atrophy was decreased among meditators.

---

31 Zorelle, "Getting Started with Mindfulness," February 18, 2019, https://zorellelife.com/1024/startmindfulness/.

"... at age fifty, brains of meditators were estimated to be 7.5 years younger.[32]

When I was in medical training, I realized that when a patient of mine was depressed, they tended to focus their attention and emotion on the past and things unresolved. I think we are all guilty of this. If we are anxious, we tend to set our focus too much in the future and the level of uncertain possibilities. When we focus in the present moments, we are better able to manage our emotional state and find a calmer and more peaceful mind. This piece of insight was extremely invaluable when I was going through the difficult times in my life. I found that if I dwell too much in the past, it robs me of my present joy, and if I worry about making the "right" decisions or what is to come, I can become almost paralyzed and can't make a decision. I have been able to withstand many hard blows in this lifetime because I learned how to turn within to speak to Spirit and allow the process to flow. I have learned how to let go and let Spirit's plan unfold. While not always easy to do, I have learned things work out for my highest good every time. Learning to trust your relationship with yourself and Spirit is a process. To begin this process, you must "learn thyself."

As we begin to delve deeper into who we are and how we are experiencing the world, let's begin to become more mindful or aware of our internal communications. An example of mindfulness is taking time to pause and evaluate what you are experiencing and why before acting or responding. Let's say you received an email at work that sparked feelings of unrest, anxiety, and even frustration. In that moment you have a choice in what you do next. You could respond immediately with an emotionally charged

---

32 Eileen Luders et al., "Estimating brain age using high-resolution pattern recognition: Younger brains in long-term meditation practitioners," *Elsevier*, (April 2016): 509–510, http://www.neuro.uni-jena.de/pdf-files/Luders-NI16.pdf.

response, which I don't recommend. This is what a lot of people do out of frustration but it typically leads to more emotionally charged emails and hurt feelings. Another alternative is to stop and evaluate what you are feeling, then honor those feelings and set them aside to determine what is really being asked and why. I typically recommend doing this to give yourself time to process what you want to say, then respond accordingly. Maybe that means taking a pause and a deep breath before you act. I have experienced this over the years, and when you can be mindful of your actions and responses, the issue can be resolved in a more satisfying way.

Meditation

The best way to listen to your intuitive mind, your higher self, God, or your guides is through meditation. Meditation has been practiced for thousands of years and has many benefits to our overall health. Stress reduction is a big result of meditation, and I believe everyone at any age can benefit from meditating just twenty minutes a day. When meditating, you are not only giving your body and mind a rest, but you are also reducing the stress-related hormone, such as cortisol, and increasing the production hormone serotonin, which helps regulate mood and social behavior, appetite and digestion, sleep, memory, and sexual desire and function. When cortisol levels are high, it causes insulin resistance, which leads to increased blood sugars, weight gain, Type 2 diabetes along with adrenal fatigue and exhaustion, and it has a negative effect on our moods.[33]

When you meditate, you are improving your immune system, reducing blood pressure, and lowering cholesterol levels. It also helps to improve the quality of your sleep. When the mind is busy

33 "Cortisol, the Stress Response, and Metabolic Markers of Stress," accessed June 9, 2020, https://wholisticmatters.com/cortisol-the-stress-response-and-metabolic-markers-of-stress/.

and cannot "shut off," it deprives us of quality and depth of sleep, causing us to feel unrestored. I see this all the time in my practice. People will come in for medication to help them sleep and are not always open to trying meditation. I recommend guided meditations for relaxation or sleep, or listening to relaxing, calming music, such as classical music, sounds of the ocean, or whatever allows you to feel in a peaceful, relaxed state while reducing caffeine and other stimulates.

The benefits of meditation are countless and far-reaching. According to a 2017 National Health Interview Survey (NHIS), the use of meditation by adults in the US tripled between 2012 and 2017 (from 4.1 percent to 14.2 percent). In US children (ages 4 to 17 years), meditation practice also increased from 0.6 percent in 2012 to 5.4 percent in 2017. The benefits improve physical conditions, mental health and overall well-being.[34] With all the many benefits of meditation, why do so few people use meditation to balance life? My patients will say, "I can't quiet my mind when I meditate," often giving up if they aren't dramatically successful after the first try. Other times they discount it as "a New Age thing." One way to ease into meditation is to take a walk in nature. Yes, walking can be a meditation, assisting us to reduce our own internal mind chatter.

There are many forms of meditation, but here are some of the most common: loving-kindness meditation, mindfulness meditation, breath-awareness meditation, kundalini yoga, Zen meditation, and transcendental meditation.[35] Each meditation has its own unique way to assist you in clearing the mind and balancing

---

34 "Meditation: In Depth," National Center for Complementary and Integrative Health, last modified April 2017, https://www.nccih.nih.gov/health/meditation-in-depth.

35 Zawn Villines, "What is the best type of meditation?" *Medical News Today*, December 22, 2017, https://www.medicalnewstoday.com/articles/320392.

the body. A key to mindfulness is to understand and honor your feelings without judgment and purposefully intend your actions and reactions to your experiences while letting go of everything else.

For loving-kindness meditation, take slow, deep breaths and open the mind to receive loving kindness, then repeatedly send messages of loving kindness to all people and the world, promoting compassion and love.

Mindfulness meditation is when you remain aware and present in the moment, encouraging you to be aware of your surroundings. This can be practiced anywhere by focusing on the sounds, sights, and smells around you. A great example of mindfulness meditation is walking in the forest. You can hear the birds, the rustling of the leaves in the wind, and smell that crisp, woodsy smell. Breathing slowly in and out will progressively relax you, as you are mindful of the sensations of your breath.

Breath-awareness meditation is a type of mindfulness that encourages you to focus on your breathing and ignore other thoughts that enter the mind or sensations felt in the body.

Kundalini yoga is a combination of deep breathing and yoga aimed to improve emotional health, physical strength, and pain reduction.

Zen meditation is part of the Buddhist practice where one focuses on postures, breathing, and mindful observation of one's thoughts without judgment. "Zen tackles deep-rooted issues and general life questions that often seem to lack answers . . ."[36]

Transcendental meditation is a spiritual form of meditation where the goal is to transcend one's current state of being, seeking heightened mindfulness or spiritual experiences. During this meditation, one can focus on breathing and repeating mantras.

36 "What Is Zen Meditation? Benefits & Techniques," Mindworks, accessed June 6, 2020, https://mindworks.org/blog/what-is-zen-meditation-benefits-techniques/.

One of my favorite meditations is called *Mediation on Twin Hearts* by Master Choa Kok Sui. This meditation is very effective in providing an overall sense of well-being and peace. The visualization asks you to picture your body like an empty vase, then pour healing colors of green and white light over your head through the entire body to every cell to the soles of the feet and out into Mother Earth.[37] Since I am very visual and colors appeal to me, this meditation is very natural. Some people find tensing their muscles and then releasing their muscles is the better way to release tension. You can do whatever feels natural to you as long as you let go of the tension.

Meditation is an invaluable tool to receive clear guidance. Meditation allows us to clear or quiet our minds, and to be more open to allow our divine guidance to come through. Whether you meditate every day or you have never meditated, it's never too late to start! Everyone has a different process, so do what feels right for you.

As you will discover, meditation is also very important when seeking the knowledge, guidance, and usable skills from the divine. It is essential when developing your psychic abilities. We must learn to rest the mind and find stillness where we can be in a state of openness. For most of us in this modern world, we run on very tight schedules, and we tend to overwork and do little self-love or self-care. These poor self-love habits clutter our minds. Meditating every day—whether it's five minutes, ten minutes, or even longer—can be transformational on how you experience daily life.

When we meditate, we raise our energetic vibrational frequency closer to that of the spirit world, and we begin to feel more connected to our higher self and Spirit. There are groups that

---

37 Master Choa Kok Sui, *Meditations for Soul Realization* (Philippines: Institute for Inner Studies, Inc., 2000), 59–72.

meditate together, various tribes and religions including Buddhist monks, Spiritualism, and Hinduism. Apps such as Insight Timer are free to download and you can meditate with people from all over the world. Group meditation "improves Group Harmony by attuning the harmonic frequency of all atoms."[38]

I have also found that meditation helps me build my relationship with my spirit helpers. I will talk with them and ask them for support and guidance. I will sit down to meditate, set my intention, and ask my guides questions or for assistance in a matter. I might ask for assistance to open my third eye and see through Spirit clearly, or to give me guidance on what to do regarding a decision. I find it's best to work one question at a time and to be as specific as possible. For example, I may say something like, "Guides, show me a clear image in my third eye regarding whether I should attend this event." Then I will take slow, deep breaths and wait for Spirit's picture.

Make sure to ask very specific questions with as many details as you can so you get the correct answer you seek. For example, if you want to know if you will meet a romantic partner at the workshop you will be attending, it may not be specific enough to just ask, "Will I meet someone at the workshop tonight?" It's likely that you will hear the answer, "Yes, you will meet people at a workshop." A more specific question would be something like, "Will I meet a romantic partner at the workshop tonight?"

Everyone will build their psychic abilities differently and in their own time. Allow yourself to begin the conversations with Spirit and your guides and see if you hear them, see images, or feel a response to your questions. Once you begin to communicate and receive messages from Spirit, you can begin to trust those messages to help guide your life.

---

38 "How Meditation Improves Group Harmony," Quantum, March 8, 2017, https://quantummeditation.co.uk/meditation-improves-group-harmony.

Exercise

Meditation is a great way to calm your body and your mind, but it does take practice. It is recommended to document what you are feeling during the meditation in your journal or in the space provided on the next page.

Mindfulness Meditation

- Begin your meditation by choosing a comfortable position. Sit in a chair or sit cross-legged on the floor or on a pillow. If you're sitting in a chair, make sure your feet are flat on the floor and rest your hands in your lap. If you are lying down, rest your arms along your sides.

- Close your eyes and begin to scan your body. Notice the stillness of your body. Relax your neck, shoulders, chest, stomach, and legs.

- Focus on your breath. Breathe in deeply through the nose, allowing the air to flow down to your stomach, and then exhale through the mouth. As you inhale, count to three. When you exhale, count to three.

- Repeat this step a few times: inhale to the count of three, then exhale to the count of three.

- Now breathe in and visualize a calming white light entering in through your nose and circulating throughout your body, healing and releasing tension and stress. As you breathe out, visualize the negative tension leaving your body.

- As you inhale and exhale, notice your thoughts or feelings. It is normal for your mind to wander, so just take notice of the thought or feeling, but don't follow it and don't let your mind pursue it. Recognize that it's simply a thought: it's what your mind does. You can notice it and then let it go.

- Picture yourself at the beach, feeling the warm sand between your toes. A light breeze blows across your face, and you smell the salty air and begin to feel relaxed.

- Imagine your thoughts and feelings are like the winds blowing. Allow them to come and let them go and just breathe.

- Spend a few minutes just soaking in the sun, feeling rejuvenated and remembering this feeling to call upon at any time in the future when you need a mental beach vacation.

- Gradually, when you are ready, bring your attention slowly back to your breath. Now begin to feel the sensations in your body and return your awareness back to the room. Gently move your fingers and toes, slowly open your eyes, and smile.

_____

_____

_____

_____

_____

_____

_____

_____

_____

_____

_____

_____

CHAPTER 7

NURTURING THE INTUITIVE SOUL

As we discover more of how intuitives are experiencing the world, we are better able to assist them to nurture self in order to assist others. One of the most important ways intuitives can show up engaged with balance in our lives is to become our *authentic self*. To tap into our authentic self, we must shift our perspective on what is important and what we value. While the term "authentic self" may be fairly new within the spiritual New Age community, the concepts are ancient. There is a common concept or belief that we come to Earth as a divine soul into this human experience to explore human life of dualities and unique tactile experiences the earth has to offer. We do this through *the veil*. This would be similar to a curtain that is many layers thick separating us from our origin on the spirit side and that of our human life. This is done by design so that we may focus on this life and the path set forth for spiritual growth and not be focused or drawn back to the joys of life on the spirit side.

In my belief, your authentic self is the ultimate soul identity before coming to Earth. The authentic self is the real you before you took human form and began changing to what you thought you should be in this lifetime. When we come into this life, we take on certain personality traits and characteristics that best assist us for what we come to experience. This differs from our authentic self, which we can think of as a loving infinite being with a higher perspective on the spirit side. These two are not separate but one that connects us to the physical and spirit side. I believe we are striving to align more with our authentic self to better understand who we truly are in the process of enlightenment. This is part of the game of life—to feel separate from our authentic self so we are free to explore Earth and have experiences. Throughout our lifetime, we will do work on self that brings us closer to our authentic self and a more peaceful, loving way of being. Those who are working the path of self-awareness, self-discovery, and transformational thoughts from self to one of unity are connecting more with their authentic self.

Now, this may be a lot to soak in, and the concept of the authentic self goes against some religious teachings. All I ask is that you keep an open mind to think about things in a new way. I didn't believe in this concept until my near-death experience showed me, and even then, it took years to understand it and integrate the knowledge.

I have always had a unique curiosity about what occurs once we transition back to the spirit side, as well as the differences of religious teachings and ideologies regarding what our authentic self is and what occurs when we pass on. I found commonalities among all Christian religions, Buddhism, and Hinduism, such as there is one Source no matter what names are used, and that we will move on to another "place" after death of the physical body. Hinduism and Buddhism believe we reincarnate into another body based on our actions in our previous life/lives. Christian religions believe there is a place determined by God based on our actions during our life on Earth for us to spend eternal life in heaven. Spiritualism believes our spirits continue to communicate with the living and continue to evolve and can continue to provide valuable information and knowledge. As the years have passed, through my own unique experiences with spirit visitations, assisting people transitioning, as well as my experience on the other side, I have learned to trust what Spirit is showing and telling me. As my insightful teacher, Reverend Elaine Thomas, says, "We are never separate; we are always connected whether we choose to look and see or not." That statement is very true! Whenever I make the conscious choice to see what is unseen it becomes clear in my vision.

Intuitives will tell you that your loved ones, angels, teachers, guides, or God are always around you, and they *always* are! So why is there separation between us on this earthly realm and our guides on a spiritual realm? My belief is that we need some separation so we can experience the things we came here to do, otherwise we will just want to spend all of our human time communicating with our loved ones over there. This is counterintuitive to our life purpose, hence the veil we all must learn to overcome and navigate. I personally find that my connection to Spirit helps me stay balanced here on Earth, and then I'm able to complete "my mission," if you will.

When I had my near-death experience, or a *choice point* experience, there was a split second after I crashed on my motorcycle from being present on Earth and then suddenly being transported elsewhere. I was suddenly in a room and felt this amazing, overwhelming feeling of love. It felt light, airy, cool, and encompassing, like being in the presence of angels. I recognized one of my guides, my maternal grandmother, who has been with me throughout this lifetime. God, or Source, was there, as well as many "onlookers," or souls, that are part of my soul family. They were offering their love and support during this "life review" as we watched the "movie" of my life up to that point. It was so profound to see how we are all connected and how we can have an effect on someone whether we know it or not. My guides showed me my blessings, such as the people who'd just showed up when I needed them, to the missed opportunities that I sidestepped untimely outcomes. I have been keeping my spirit helpers a lot busier than I thought!

But it wasn't all positive. I was shown some very painful and hurtful experiences that had happened in my life. They showed me the sad times when I felt alone, my failed marriage, and things I've said that hurt other people. I saw and felt different heartbreaks when people I loved died, my stubbornness, and the choices I've made. As we all sat in this room, as if in a movie theater, I asked, "Why would anyone choose to experience such suffering? There is no way I would choose this." They just looked at me with such loving gazes and tried to help me understand. My guides told me that I chose all of my experiences for my *soul growth*, which was a concept I could not grasp at the time.

Then one of the guides moved closer to sit beside me and touched my shoulder. "It is okay, we want you to understand," my guide said. Suddenly, the movie started up again, and I saw another version of myself as a beautiful, brilliant body of white light standing in a similar room around a table. There was a big table with lots of pieces laid out like a board game of life, and there were other people there, such as my neighbor Bernie in her white-light body. They were all talking in what seemed like a strategy session, planning to come in at different times during my life to assist with different issues I would face. I started to cry, knowing somehow this was all true. It was at that moment when I started to look at my personal movie in a completely different way, where I was not the victim of my circumstance but a tiny part of the master plan.

Then another guide came forth and sat beside me. He discussed that I needed to choose to get back on the path. He told me that I was not listening to Spirit's signs and words, and that I wanted to come into this lifetime to experience certain things for my soul growth. "You are getting in the way of your own happiness."

He was right; I did feel as if I was missing something inside. I was not certain if I had died, but I wanted to stay because I felt such unconditional love. He said, "You have a choice." I could stay in the spirit realm, or I could go back to my life and complete what I came to Earth to do. After much discussion with my guides, I agreed to return to Earth, but I needed help and wanted everything in my life to change and put me in alignment with my purpose. Boy oh boy, be careful proclaiming that to the universe!

And in a split second I was back in my body, which had sustained pretty significant injuries that required a year and a half of surgeries and physical therapies to regain most functioning of my physical body. It took me years to process on the emotional and spiritual levels. This is what I call my "spiritual time out." I had a time out so I could process all I had seen and felt on the other side while trying to finish my master's degree in nursing and care for my loyal companion, Cooper, a German Shephard with degenerative lesions on his spine. Spirit gave me the time and space to begin to heal years of issues in my tissues through energy work, therapy, and reconnecting with Spirit through mediumship and meditation.

I share this experience to demonstrate that sometimes we have to go through a process of dramatic change to peel away the layers of "stuff" we have collected in our human form so we can begin to rediscover our true authentic self. During this process, it brought into question all the beliefs and values I was holding on to. This challenged my thoughts on death, the afterlife, a life review, divine beings helping us, and the religious teachings I studied over the years.

During that time in my life, I wasn't sure what I believed occurred in the afterlife. But through all of my spirit communications, I understood somehow that loved ones can still communicate with us—I just didn't understand the mechanics. I did believe that when we pass to the spirit realm, there would be a life review to help us see ourselves, but I wasn't sure what occurred after that. I also believed angels were always with us with their loving energies, and that was confirmed. Immediately after my near-death experience, some of my beliefs were verified, but others were still unclear. It took years to debate these topics with myself until I determined I needed to gather more information, and I asked for spiritual guidance.

At some point in our lives, we all begin to question our purpose in life. Whenever I begin to question my beliefs, my thoughts, and my actions, I reflect and realign myself moving forward in the path of what I want. Becoming your authentic self is that same process of self-discovery and allowing yourself to learn what is different from what you thought and to then move in that direction. As we grow and mature through life experiences, it is natural to gain different perspectives. The beauty and freedom you gain by allowing yourself this process is invaluable. Allowing myself to gather more information through spiritual workshops, books, study groups; and conversations with self, other people, and Spirit offered the most comprehensive database of knowledge to decide what felt most in alignment to my soul. This path led me to become a Spiritualist who is always seeking to gain understanding of both the physical and spiritual worlds.

There are many benefits in following the flow of the authentic-self process. For example, making decisions is a lot easier when you realize that you do have choices. When you do the things that will make you happy, you will gain more fulfillment, and your self-awareness increases as does increased alignment with your goals and dreams and self-love. One way to begin to understand yourself better and what is important in your life is to understand what you value, what drives you, what inspires you, and what you enjoy.

In Table 1 on the next page, select the top ten values that

resonate with you. Write them in your journal and reflect on them daily. Change them if you feel guided, and acknowledge why they have changed.[39]

TABLE 1

Authenticity	Abundance	Beauty	Balance
Compassion	Confidence	Courage	Creativity
Communication	Calm	Determination	Excellence
Fun	Friendship	Family	Gratitude
Growth	Generosity	Honesty	Health
Happiness	Harmony	Independence	Intuition
Integrity	Joy	Love	Listening
Loyalty	Optimism	Open-mindedness	Peace
Productivity	Passion	Patience	Respect
Service	Success	Strength	Spirituality
Simplicity	Tradition	Transparency	Thankfulness
Trust	Understanding	Wisdom	Wealth

Now that you are exploring what you value, ask yourself if you are doing the things that you love. Do you love your job? What do you love about yourself? What do you love about your life? What do you want to do differently? What is your purpose in life? What will it take to get in alignment with your purpose?

Spend some time with these questions and others that may come up. You will not have all the answers. One of the hardest things is just sitting with ourselves and getting real with our feelings and thoughts. The intensity of the emotions that can arise doing this work can be very painful. People may experience fear, anxiety, sadness, grief, loss of self or others, embarrassment, shame, guilt, or anger. Most people will only get so far in this process

39 "What Are Your Values? Deciding What's Most Important in Life," MindTools, accessed June 9, 2020, https://www.mindtools.com/pages/article/newTED_85.htm.

and quit because it can be painful to peel away the raw wounds of what needs to be healed, to actually do the work to heal, and to eventually let go. But the work is always worth doing! If you want the life you feel you are meant to experience, you have to discover the things within you that need to be healed. You have to do the work to heal and let go of aspects of your life to make room for the new to come in.

An important thing to remember on this path to discovering your authentic self is to have a sense of humor about the whole process. This can be very heavy emotionally to explore, and it is very important to laugh at yourself as you grow through the process. There is a famous quote often attributed to Socrates: "To know thyself is the beginning of wisdom." I believe self-love is wisdom in action. One way we can assist in our healing is to start by loving ourselves, and only then will our life experiences be in alignment with our authentic self. Self-love allows us to feel more of the love from the spirit side of life. When we connect with our loving nature, we are more in alignment with our authentic self and Spirit. You can enhance all aspects of your life when you feel connected to Spirit and yourself.

Self-love is the appreciation for yourself that grows from actions that support the growth of your body, mind, and spirit. When we nurture our love of self, we begin to accept our weaknesses as well as our strengths. We begin to show compassion to ourselves and others for our human struggle. We begin to be more grateful for the little things and find more personal meaning to our experiences. This self-love allows us to feel more centered in our values and life purpose, which ultimately allows us to live a more fulfilling life through our own making. It can also help you to strengthen your psychic abilities through your strengthened connection with self and spirit.

Here are four ways you can practice self-love:[40]

Practice good self-care. Meeting your basic needs is not enough. You need to care for your body, mind, and spirit. Eat healthy and nutritious foods, exercise regularly, get the proper amount of sleep, and interact in healthy relationships. Try activities such as massage, acupuncture, exercise classes, gym memberships, development circles, or whatever you feel called to do that is enhancing your human experience.

Set boundaries. You need to set clear boundaries with everyone you interact with. This can be a challenge for some people, especially when it comes to family members. It is important to identify and remove unhealthy patterns that are not helping your spiritual path. Set limits and learn that "no" is a complete sentence. If someone or something is depleting you physically, emotionally, or spiritually, you are allowing the unhealthy boundary.

Develop your self-awareness. Understanding who you are, and what you think, feel, and want in life empowers you to live a more mindful and fulfilled life. Living mindfully allows you the freedom to pursue your own goals and dreams and not what others want for you. You can live your life intentionally to the purpose that you are creating and designing for you.

Act purposefully. This is when you can identify the difference between being "wanty" and "needy," as I like to call it. Humans tend to be very "wanty" and want everything yesterday. The reality is that we need very little to truly be in joy. When we act on what

---

40 Deborah Khoshaba, "A Seven-Step Prescription for Self-Love," *Psychology Today*, March 27, 2012, https://www.psychologytoday.com/us/blog/get-hardy/201203/seven-step-prescription-self-love.

we *need* rather than what we *want*, we are able to stay focused in the present. Learning to keep focused and turn away from old-patterned behaviors that keep us stuck in the past improves our self-love.

Exercise

This exercise will help you acknowledge a *need* versus a *want*. Oftentimes, we can mistake the two without even realizing it. For example: We *need* to exercise, but we *want* a gym membership. We know it's healthy to exercise, but buying a gym membership is a luxury.

When you can examine the ways you care for yourself and distinguish whether something is a need or a want, you are better able to nurture yourself as well as those around you.

- Write a list of five things in your life that make you feel happy and fulfilled. (Example: exercise, religion, reading, family.)

- Write one or two sentences about how each thing brings joy and fulfillment to your life.

- Now label each thing as a *need* or a *want*.

_____

_____

_____

_____

_____

_____

_____

_____

_____

_____

_____

_____

_____

Exercise

We can all make small changes in our lives to practice self-love. Over the next week, here are three things you can do each day that will help improve your mood and get you on the path of practicing self-love. You can pick one, two, or all three, or you can choose your own tasks. The key is to be consistent and do it each day.

- Before breakfast, meditate for five minutes to set a positive intention of improved health and vitality.
- Drink eight (or more) glasses of water each day.
- Go outside for ten minutes each day. You can take a walk or just sit on your porch.

After one week, how do you feel? Did your mood improve each morning after meditating? Did your body feel different after hydrating with water? Self-love doesn't come easy or even natural for some people, so implementing small changes into your daily routine will help you stay focused.

_____

_____

_____

_____

_____

_____

_____

_____

_____

_____

_____

_____

_____

_____

_____

_____

_____

_____

_____

_____

CHAPTER 8

ATTITUDE OF GRATITUDE

The saying, "Start each day with a grateful heart," really touches my soul. I believe that starting each day in gratitude sets the intention for the day. I begin my days with breathing exercises, and then I meditate on affirmations of gratitude and my connection with Spirit. By doing this, I'm opening myself up to receive messages and inspiration from Spirit. This allows me to get out of my busy mind that wants to plan and achieve all the goals and things I pile onto my plate every day. Have you noticed that the older we get, the more we tend to think we can accomplish in one day?

We are energetic beings that are exposed to various stressors and environmental toxins that can decrease our vibrational frequency. Positive thoughts, such as gratitude, increase our vibrational frequency, and when we increase this energetic resonance, we improve our immune system, strengthen our auric field, and improve our overall well-being. A 2003 study conducted by Robert A. Emmons and Michael E. McCullough sought to discover whether having gratitude, or "counting your blessings," has a psychological benefit. In one study, there were two groups: a gratitude group and a control group. Participants were given a packet of sixteen "daily experience rating forms" that focused on things such as "daily mood," "health report," and gratitude. Participants were asked to keep track of things such as daily exercise, the number of caffeinated beverages consumed, and how many hours they slept, etc. The gratitude-outlook groups showed heightened well-being in several areas. "The effect on positive affect appeared to be the most robust finding. Results suggest that a conscious focus on blessings may have emotional and interpersonal benefits."[41]

When we practice gratitude, our brain is flooded with dopamine, which is the chemical that produces a natural euphoric feeling. Exercise releases endorphins producing similar effects. A consistent practice of gratitude releasing dopamine reduces mental health disorders such as anxiety and depression. It is thought to improve our conscious awareness, peace, and joy as it allows us to become more in alignment with our authentic self. Studies by Giacomo Bono show that the use of gratitude promotes strength of caring and compassion for social interactions, strengthens the connection and character of moral functions, and improves motivation and self-improvement in fostering positive youth development. It was also discovered that grateful people are found to be more satisfied with life overall, have more hope; less depression, anxiety, or envy; more empathy, and are forgiving and supportive toward others.[42]

There are many ways to practice gratitude. I have found a daily practice to be the most beneficial. Start by being in the present moment and notice the smallest of things about your environment. Can you see the beauty around you? Do you notice the birds chirping in the morning, or the smile of a stranger, your health, the roof over your head, or a beautiful sunrise? When you can begin to be still and just listen and look and really see the beauty

41 Robert A. Emmons et al., "Count Blessings Versus Burdens: An Experimental Investigation of Gratitude and Subjective Well-Being in Daily Life," *Journal of Personality and Social Psychology*, vol. 84, no. 2 (2003), 377–389, doi: 10.1037/0022-3514.84.2.377.

42 Giacomo Bono et al., "The Power and Practice of Gratitude," in *Positive Psychology in Practice* (Hoboken: John Wiley & Sons, Inc., 2015), 561, https://onlinelibrary.wiley.com/doi/abs/10.1002/9781118896874.ch33.

around you, you can begin to feel grateful. During the dark times in my life, I would struggle to see the positive, but I would force myself to see one positive thing I could give thanks for that day. Some days were tough, but I always found at least one thing to be grateful for. It could be that I had food on the table, or that my dog didn't roll around in the mud in the yard. Begin to see the magic that is all around you.

Another great way to feel the gratitude in your body is to communicate it to those around you. When you can tell someone what you appreciate about them or how they contribute to your life experience, it demonstrates kindness and compassion. Smile and express your warmth with the person you first interact with in your day, family, friends, strangers, or pets. The point is to share your *beautiful heart with others. I truly enjoy when a simple, genuine* compliment brightens someone's face and ripples more positivity with everyone he or she interacts with. When you can express gratitude for others around you, it can shift their entire day. We all know someone who complains all day long and doesn't understand why everything is so negative in their perspective. I enjoy doing nice things and demonstrating gratitude for them in my life. It's what I like to call the "attitude of gratitude." Demonstrating love and compassion through gratitude allows us to be closer to our authentic self. Love is what makes us all thrive.

One suggestion is to keep a gratitude journal or jar, and then revisit your jar at the end of the month, or the end of the year if you're feeling ambitious. I have a gratitude jar, and around four in the afternoon, when my workday is winding down, I write down one to three things or people I am grateful for. At the end of the year, I go through the jar to see the people and things I most appreciated. This is a fun thing to do! On some of the days, I wrote that I was grateful to go to bed. It must have been a really stressful day for me to write that. I do have a sense of humor, even on the rough days! When we allow ourselves to feel gratitude daily, the universe attracts more things into our reality to be grateful for. Over time I began to notice my attention was focusing more on the blessings in a situation and things that were going right than focusing on what was going wrong. I began to feel less stressed at work and home and have a deeper level of flexibility to life situations.

One of the best ways to love yourself and increase gratitude for our humanness is through forgiveness. Forgiveness for self and others is a very powerful tool. We are so very hard on ourselves and tend to try to take on everyone else's issues, and then we punish ourselves for being overwhelmed or make mistakes in the growing process. It is fascinating to observe people and watch these dynamics play out. As intelligent as humans are, we rarely see we cause a lot of the issues ourselves. Learning to accept our dualities of strengths and weaknesses, positive and negative experiences, and that we are not perfect but perfectly flawed, is the key to self-forgiveness. There are never mistakes, just lessons learned, or in many cases, relearned. Learning to find humor in my human experiences has helped me to see beauty in the imperfections.

It is my hope that we all find resolution of conflict and unresolved issues, and find peace while we walk this earth. Forgiveness can be a challenge for many people. We've been hurt or wronged and need to forgive, or we have wronged and hurt and we need someone to forgive us. *Ho'oponopono* (ho-o-pono-pono) is "the Hawaiian practice of reconciliation and forgiveness."[43] It's a very powerful tool to shift energies and assist healing. The ancient Hawaiian culture believed that illness was caused by breaking spiritual laws and that illness could not be cured until the sufferer atoned for this transgression and sought forgiveness.[44]

---

43 "*Ho'oponopono*," Wikipedia, last modified July 5, 2020, https://en.wikipedia.org/wiki/Ho%CA%BBoponopono.

44 Ibid.

Today *Ho'oponopono* is used to clear life situations, places, relationships, and financial situations by getting to the source of the trouble and by accepting 100 percent responsibility for that and repeating the process. No guilt trip, no intellectualizing, no judgment.

I have used *ho'oponopono* in different situations in my life that I didn't have a full understanding of, but I could palpably feel the shift in energy around the people and situations. I used this process with a family member. No matter what I said or did, she and I could not seem to find common ground, and we would continuously engage in disagreements that would end in hurt feelings. I practiced *ho'oponopono* every night by talking to a picture of my family member, as we were not able to communicate for more than five minutes without one of us becoming upset. After one month, I noticed she began to soften her tone of voice when communicating, and I was not as reactive in interactions. After three months, I was no longer reacting in a negative way to her and was beginning to understand why she was behaving a certain way, and we were able to have communication for longer than five minutes without a disagreement.

There are many ways to practice gratitude, but the best place to start would be to look inward. Think about how grateful you are to wake up every morning and that your heart is beating and your body is able to move. Think about how grateful you are to have a roof over your head, and food on your table. When you can find gratitude in your daily life, you can extend that gratitude outward to all living things.

Exercise

Usually, the *ho'oponopono* practice is performed with a partner. It is believed to work better when you can look each other in the eye, but if you are not able to work directly with someone, you can ask their higher self and your higher self to sit together and work the issues out. You could also use a photograph of the person, just like I did in my example with my relative.

Before you begin this practice, say a prayer for Spirit to assist this process or whatever you feel called to say. Everyone involved is expected to cooperate to work on their problems. You must allow for periods of silence and reflection to deal with emotions or injuries that arise.

- Sit in a comfortable position across from your partner.

- Make a statement about the problem or issue you are having. Be honest about how you feel, even if it is painful or hurtful.

- Next, your partner will discuss how they feel and their own issues. Be open and understanding when your partner is honest about his or her feelings, which can be painful and hurtful to you.

- Confession, repentance, and forgiveness take place. You are considered clean and divinity will do the rest.

- Repeat the following phrase out loud like a mantra: "I love you, please forgive me, I am sorry, thank you."[45] You and your partner can take turns saying it or you can say it in unison. This cleaning process ignites the self-transformation process and is repeated as many times as you feel is needed to clean the issues between you and your partner. As you breathe in and out, you clean your body from the "polluted" air and enrich it with fresh, oxygen-rich air.

- The ceremony is complete when you feel that you can let the issue, the situation, or the person go with forgiveness and move forward.

---

45 Ibid.

- Close the ceremony in prayer and gratitude to Spirit, the person, the issue, or the situation, and for the healing that occurred for all.

The *ho'oponopono* process takes practice. You may find peace after one session, but it can take multiple sessions. When you feel a shift in the way you feel, you are healing, just continue to repeat the phrase. When I was going through this process, I felt a feeling of calm come over my body and more love in my heart the more I repeated the mantra. It is recommended to document your feelings in your journal or in the space below.

_____

_____

_____

_____

_____

_____

_____

_____

_____

_____

Exercise

Keep a gratitude journal or jar for thirty days. Write down one to three things or people you are grateful for every day. At the end of the thirty days, review what you have written down. Take notice of the patterns, which people you are truly grateful for, and for your growth of being more present. If you enjoyed this exercise for thirty days, try doing it longer, maybe for six months or for a year.

_____

_____

_____

_____

_____

_____

_____

_____

_____

_____

_____

_____

_____

_____

_____

CHAPTER 9

THE UNIVERSAL LAWS

The Universal Laws, or the universal truths, are thought to govern the way the universe works. While humans do not come with an operation manual, we do have these fantastic laws that teach us valuable lessons. Their origin is unknown and don't belong to any religion or spiritual tradition. They apply to everything and everybody like other laws of nature. They were created together with the universe by the universal consciousness, the infinite Spirit or God, and have been passed through generations through various spiritual teachers.

We can use these Universal Laws to create the life we came here to experience. For me, practicing self-awareness daily and teaching my development students the process of self-awareness is vital to living a more fulfilled life. We need to first become conscious of our thoughts, words, and deeds if we are to change them for ones more in alignment of what we are trying to create.

The most discussed Universal Law is the Law of Attraction. The *Law of Attraction* is the belief that we attract what we think, regardless of whether it's positive or negative. It is perhaps one of the more exciting laws due to its direct effect of producing positive aspects of life. But the other Universal Laws are just as important, as they can help you navigate certain areas of your life:[46]

---

46 Sarah Regan, "The 12 Universal Laws & How to Practice Them," April 16, 2020, https://www.mindbodygreen.com/articles/the-12-universal-laws-and-how-to-practice-them.

Universal Laws

The *Law of Divine Oneness* teaches us cause and effect, and that everything is interconnected.

The *Law of Vibration* teaches us that the entire universe and everything in it is made up of energy and carries a unique vibration.

The *Law of Inspired Action* teaches us purposeful action as we manifest the things our actions support.

The *Law of Correspondence* teaches us about communication between ourselves on Earth and our higher self in the spirit world.

The *Law of Cause and Effect* teaches us accountability for our actions and consequences.

The *Law of Compensation* teaches us about abundance.

The *Law of Attraction* teaches us that we manifest what we focus on.

The *Law of Perpetual Transmutation of Energy* teaches us that mindfulness can transform your life.

The *Law of Relativity* teaches personal growth through challenges.

The *Law of Polarity* teaches transformation through opposites.

The *Law of Rhythm* teaches non-attachment as life moves in cycles.

The *Law of Gender* teaches balance in all things.

As energetic beings, we need to become aware of our feelings and sensations in our body and mind. Become aware of when you are allowing energy to flow or when you are blocking it. Learn to understand what you are "feeling." Are you feeling negative emotions—fear, sadness, judgment, anger—that are bringing your vibration down?

Your role is to identify the misalignment or negative feelings, not condemn yourself. I have learned to get a good sense of humor with others and myself. Once you identify these feelings, you are then able to shift your perspective and raise your vibration. Changing your physiology changes your focus through a shift in physical positioning or mental redirection. Raise your vibration by walking in nature, listening to music, salt baths, spending time with friends: whatever makes your soul happy. At that point, you are better able to see where you want to make change.

Becoming aware of your habitual thoughts that manifest into things and circumstances will also help you see what you want to change. Begin to see what you want to replace the thought, emotion, and circumstance with and play with the energy drawing it to your reality. Then you need to let the negative things go with love and replace those with people, places, things, or thoughts *you are trying to create in your life. If you enjoy being with like*-minded people who participate in a particular activity, then focus on how you can attract more of that. Are there places close to you that host these activities? Begin to change the things that are not serving your highest good or your shift in vision, and before long you will be living the life you desire.

When I think about these laws, I reflect on my life experiences and can begin to understand when I was and was not in the flow of the universe. As a young woman in my twenties, I was using the Law of Attraction and not even knowing it. Even if we do not understand these laws, we are still using them. It is important to use them purposefully for our life experiences and spiritual growth. This would be like betting everything you have on a game you don't know the rules to and just jumping in and allowing whatever outcome to occur.

Like many of us, I used to have the poor-me attitude. I would question "why me" because everything appeared to be such a challenge when things didn't go smoothly. I noticed that when things were going wrong, it was the only thing on my radar. Even when something good occurred, I would say things like, "It won't last and something worse is coming." This was the type of internal communication I had with myself, and life would demonstrate or mirror it, which would just reinforce this thought process. This cycle repeated, and it was not until one day someone asked me if I really felt that hopeless. I paused. I would not have described myself as *hopeless*, so I was forced to reflect on what that meant to me. I always thought I was a pretty positive person, but when I observed my own communication and interactions, I could see the negative communication. Then I noticed that the people around me were also complaining all day long about everything as well. After a week of intense observing myself, I realized that I could change this, but I needed to find out how.

I asked Spirit to let me know every time I spoke or thought in a negative way. Then I took notice of people who spoke positively, such as Wayne Dyer and Louise Hay. The way they looked at life and situations inspired hope and love in my heart. I knew instantly this was something I could do with practice. So, I wrote in my journal when I noticed myself saying something negative about myself or something else. It was eye-opening. You'd be surprised how many negative thoughts you have on a daily basis. Every time I had a negative thought, I immediately turned it into a positive. For example, when I would make a mistake, I would say how stupid I was to make the same mistake again. Once I began to notice the knee-jerk reaction to say I was stupid, I would replace that negative thought with, "It was not a big deal, and you will be more aware in the future so you don't repeat the same outcome." This grew over time, and before I knew it, I was monitoring myself without much effort. I noticed more positive things in my life as my thoughts and communication changed. I began to find gratitude for the little things in my life. I became more present in my interactions with others, which allowed me to see people in a more empathetic way. This is a powerful way for spiritual growth to occur.

As the saying goes, hindsight is 20/20, and we can learn great lessons by noticing our patterns and then adjusting our thoughts and actions so we are moving forward. It is always interesting to discover the catalyst for such transformational change. For me, it was one person just expressing what they interpreted about me—that I was too negative—to cause such life-changing effects. We never know what we might say or do that can make someone else become aware of their own actions. I believe we must take the time to do our own spiritual work to grow and evolve. So many of us have created very busy lives full of responsibilities and duties, and we don't spend time on ourselves or value our needs as a priority. If we are to be the best we can be, then we must take the time every day to show up for ourselves.

Spending time evaluating how we are using the Universal Laws can afford us great perspective on how we are living our lives. Once we begin a daily practice of evaluation, we allow ourselves to improve our gratitude and satisfaction in our interactions. I enjoy journaling for ten to twenty minutes at the end of my day to reflect and evaluate how I used the Universal Laws.

By purposefully using the Law of Attraction to think positively, we attract more positivity into our lives. Mindfully using the Law of Perpetual Transmutation of Energy to let go at the end of the day allows you to shift perspective and align more with your authentic self. I enjoy the process of body scanning daily and purposefully reassessing myself as I move throughout the day in hopes to be more mindful and self-aware of my thoughts, words, and actions. Noticing how I am experiencing my day assists me to self-correct in real time, increasing my vibration, and improving my mood and ultimately my day. The Universal Laws will help you learn to master mindfulness or self-awareness to your energy, thoughts, words, and reactions, and produce positive outcomes in your daily life. I encourage you to begin a process of self-awareness, and document your experience to help you understand the process and yourself better. Most of all, have a good sense of humor about yourself and the way you experience the world.

Exercise

This exercise will help you examine how much you are aware of the ways you are using the Universal Laws. This is a way to evaluate how you are interacting in the world. Allow yourself to see all aspects of yourself without judgment. You will need your journal for this exercise.

- Choose one Universal Law to focus on.
- Write down two examples of how you can put this law into practice in your life. For example, evaluate your work–life balance with the Law of Gender. Are you working too many hours and not spending enough time with family? If so, you would write something like, "I am working seventy hours a week and do not have time for other things."
- Evaluate your example and come up with a solution of how the law can help you in this situation. For example, if you are working too many hours at work and not spending enough time with family, what can you do to rectify that? You could write, "I am working seventy hours a week, so I need to tell my boss that I can only work late on Tuesdays so I can have more time to spend with my family."
- Repeat with another Universal Law.

CHAPTER 10

LIVING WITH INTENTION

We all know someone who goes through life on a mission with plans and goals and is driven to continuously move toward their goal. Some might say this person is most likely successful in life, has a thriving career, a happy marriage, is able to travel for leisure, and can purchase things they desire. Then we also know the person who just goes with the flow allowing life to throw whatever it wants at them. They tend to not follow goals or be very ambitious. The difference, however, is that the goal-driven person is most likely utilizing a daily practice of intention setting to achieve success.

Intention is the starting point for everything you want to manifest in your life. The best way I can explain this is a New Year's resolution. A week before, or even the night before the new year, you think about the things you want to be different or the things you want to accomplish in the coming year. You set your intention to work toward goals of some kind. The goals can be long-term, such as wanting to lose twenty pounds over the next six months. They can also be short-term, such as drinking eight glasses of water every day. The mindful setting of the intention is the driving force behind the goal. Beginning each day with an intention is a very easy yet powerful way to conspire with the universe to create what you want for that day! If your goals are to lose weight over the longer term, you need to make daily changes. For example, a daily intention could be to drink eight glasses of water a day *and* eat fresh vegetables and fruits with healthy lean meat options.

I intend to feel my optimal best throughout the day with strong energy and feelings of vitality. I like to start my day with intention setting, affirmations on how I want to work with Spirit, then meditation, and then sharing Spirit-inspired guidance for the day through live broadcasting on social media. I set intentions by asking Spirit to guide my thoughts, words, and actions for the highest good of all I come in contact with. I ask to be a vessel for the divine to work through me as we serve Spirit in my practice. I may also ask for specific Spirit members, such as my healing guides, to assist the care I provide in my practice. This process may look different for you, but make sure it's something that resonates with you.

Having a consistent practice helps you to be the most successful. There are days that I am running late, so I'll shorten the duration I spend doing each activity instead of skipping them. If I skip my intention or any activity, I tend to feel more scattered, less grounded, and little things will shift my energy. I get overwhelmed easily in the energy of others. The best part is if I notice these subtle changes, I can spend a few minutes redirecting myself. Depending on the circumstance, I may set a different intention, do a few affirmations, or fit in a five- to ten-minute meditation, and like magic I am regrouped, refreshed, and ready to begin again. I cannot stress enough the importance of having some type of intention practice on a daily basis, especially with the hustle-and-bustle of our daily lives.

If I notice myself becoming short or easily irritated by other people, I will go into a room by myself and take a few minutes for a few deep breaths. I will ask Spirit to assist me in feeling calm, centered, and full of love and divine light. This works by removing myself from whatever was irritating me and allows me to breathe and realign my intention with Spirit. You must do what you feel called to do and what works best for you. Remember that tools may change over time, where one day taking a few deep breaths is all you need to redirect your energy, but other days it may take multiple affirmations, meditations, and breathing. An easy way to begin a daily practice is to learn to center yourself.

As mentioned, meditation has many benefits, and I love my daily meditation practice. As you meditate, make note of what you are experiencing—sensing, feeling, hearing, and seeing—and set that aside. Think about what you want for your day. I like to set the intention of what makes my day feel good. Since my day consists of seeing patients, I set my intention to help all those who come to me for healing. I also ask to be a clear vessel for the divine to work *through me, allowing all those I come in contact with to receive* what they need for their highest good. I set the intention to call in my specialized spirit helpers from across the veil to work with me for healing of all. I also ask Spirit to set a column of white light that they will monitor around me from the heavens to the center of Mother Earth and continuously nourish us both in a flow of divine light. This is the most effective way I have found to do my work without being overly influenced by other people's energies.

Learning to live your life with intention is not only being purposeful with your thoughts and words, but it is also about reinforcing those intentions through your senses. A vision board can be a useful tool for setting intentions and assisting you in manifesting what you want in your life. A vision board is a visual reminder of the things you want to manifest in your life or your vision for your future.

I love working with vision boards. It's such a creative way for me to express myself. I create a type of collage with photographs, words, and other inspiring images. The idea is to create an intention for yourself and what you want to manifest. I like to place my vision boards in a visual place, such as next to my workspace, where I will see it on a daily basis. It really is that simple. When you see it every day—even if you don't acknowledge it with interaction— your intuitive mind will pick up those items and reinforce your desired intention. I enjoy teaching children to use vision boards because it helps them to learn to take responsibility for purposeful intention for what they are experiencing in life.

Another way to facilitate your intentions is through your connection and interactions with Spirit. Imagine having Spirit help you navigate every decision you make. It's mind-blowing to think about, but that is exactly what you can do. Spirit wants to assist us in any way that we need . . . we just have to ask. We always try to complicate things, but it's really that simple.

It's important to be in contact with your Spirit helpers, and the more you practice, the easier it will be. If you have highly developed psychic abilities, you could just ask and receive the information in whatever way you receive through vision, hearing, and feeling. But if you have not yet developed those skills, using a pendulum is a great way to assist you in receiving the information.

According to the *Merriam-Webster Dictionary*, a *pendulum* is "a weight hung from a point so as to swing freely back and forth under the action of gravity."[47] A pendulum is a useful tool to communicate with Spirit. It can be made of any material. For instance, you could tie a nut to a piece of string. In the New Age community, pendulums are often made from gemstones.

Let's say you need help to reach your intended goal of running a marathon. You could ask Spirit to help you decide what is the best way for you to train. Utilizing this skill can help you achieve whatever you want with less unwanted outcomes. It's like phoning

---

47 *Merriam-Webster Dictionary*, s.v. "pendulum," accessed June 10, 2020, https://www.merriam-webster.com/dictionary/pendulum.

a friend on that gameshow, *Who Wants to Be a Millionaire*, or getting an inside tip to the big game of life.

By using a pendulum to receive answers from Spirit, you can better set your intentions and manifest the desired things in your life. This process is known as *dowsing*. According to Sig Lonegren, author of *The Pendulum Kit*, *dowsing* is "the scientific art that interprets the movements of a swinging pendulum to find answers to questions."[48]

When working with a pendulum, only ask *yes* and *no* questions. I always begin each use of a pendulum by placing the string in-between my right thumb and first finger and hold the pendulum suspended over the palm of my left hand. I allow it to be still and suspended. Then I ask the pendulum, "Show me a *yes*." I wait for the pendulum to move in one direction. For me this typically is vertical over my left palm. Then I say, "Show me a *no*," and wait for the pendulum to move in another direction. For me this is typically circular in a clockwise position over my left palm.

I allow the pendulum to stop and hover over my left palm. Then I ask my *yes* or *no* question and wait for the pendulum to move over my hand. This is how I know what answer will be demonstrated. I start with setting the intention by asking permission from Spirit to work this way and see what I receive. If my pendulum moves in the way it demonstrated *yes*, then I say thank you so Spirit knows I have received the message. I say a prayer asking for the highest vibrational Spirit guidance and protection of the highest light.

I wait for my pendulum to come back to hovering and proceed to my next question. I usually like to ask, "Is this the truth?" and see how the pendulum moves. If yes, I will continue to my next question. If no, I will stop and reset the intention to only work with the highest vibrational Spirits. Only once did the pendulum

---

48 Sig Lonegren, *The Pendulum Kit* (New York: Atria Publishing, 1990), 6.

give me repeated no's, and I immediately stopped working with it. There are "trickster energies," or low vibrational spirits, who like to interfere, and I refuse to work with them and recommend you do not either. I will then ask my questions and watch which way the pendulum swings. I tend to ask the same question in different ways to ensure consistency.

Let's put this pendulum swinging to use. Let's say I want to know if I will meet my future husband at a spiritual workshop. I will ask the pendulum a variety of questions in the same vein: *Will I meet someone at the workshop? Will I meet a romantic partner at the workshop? Will I meet someone I am interested in at the workshop? Will I meet someone who is interested in me at the workshop? Will I meet someone who is ready to be in a romantic relationship at the workshop? Will I meet my future husband at this workshop?* All of these questions can give me different answers. The pendulum might say that I will meet my future husband at the workshop, and the pendulum might say that I won't meet someone who is ready to be in a relationship. Both could be correct. You could meet your future husband but he won't be ready to be in a relationship or even be interested in you at the current moment. Maybe he is fresh out of a relationship and not even noticing women right now. Asking different questions can provide you with a bigger picture or understanding of the question you seek answers to.

One time, I used a pendulum in a really fun way. I gifted my nieces and nephews each with their own pendulum and taught them how to use it. Then they went from room to room asking questions until they found their Christmas present. No matter how you choose to work with Spirit on your intentions, you need to learn to trust your instincts and the guidance you receive. I like to ask Spirit questions and see what my intuition sees, feels, and hears. If I am in doubt, I'll use pendulums to confirm. Interacting with Spirit daily can help you live in the present moment while being mindful of your words, thoughts, and actions. It allows me to get out of the way and allow the divine to work through me. Allowing ourselves to play with new skills opens us up to the magic.

Exercise

Create a vision board to set an intention(s). The key is to make sure that your intention is clear, focused, and specific. For example, "I want to lose five pounds every two weeks," is a clear-set intention. It is also realistic. Avoid vague intentions, such as, "I want to lose weight this month," or an unrealistic intention, such as, "I want to lose twenty pounds in one week." The more honest and focused you are in your intention, the more likely you are to achieve it.

I like to create a vision board in January to start the new year and then revaluate it in July. You can do a shorter duration, though it is suggested to do this for a minimum of one month.

- Make an intention about what you want to manifest in your life.

- Use a large piece of cardboard or a small piece of paper for your base. Note: you can also create a virtual vision board on your smartphone or device, or on a bigger canvas such as a wall.

- Use photographs of family and loved ones, words that inspire you, and other images or pictures that you want to keep close and bring into your reality. For example, use photographs or places where you want to travel if your intention is to backpack in Scotland at the end of the summer.

- Place your vision board where you will see it daily.

- Journal about your vision board every month to evaluate desired manifestations.

_____

_____

_____

_____

_____

_____

_____

_____

_____

_____

_____

_____

Exercise

In this exercise, you will learn how to set a daily intention and how to evaluate your progress. Do this exercise every day for one week. You can always work your way up to thirty days or longer.

Sometimes it's very helpful to visually see your progress. Maybe you notice that you have trouble completing your intention on Wednesdays, and then you can evaluate why that is. I suggest starting small with one intention, but feel free to do more. Over time, it becomes easier to realign with your intentions using self-awareness and mindfulness.

- Set one intention in the morning. For example, your intention is to be in a calm state of being all day.

- At the end of the day, review your intention and write down all the ways in which you *succeeded* in your intention. For example, you remained calm in traffic by practicing deep breathing.

- Next, write down all the ways in which you were *not successful* in your intention. What happened in your day that caused you to not be calm? (Maybe you had to wait extra long at a doctor's office, etc.)

_____

_____

_____

_____

_____

_____

_____

_____

_____

_____

_____

_____

_____

CHAPTER 11

WORKING WITH DIVINE BEINGS

The best part about learning to work with Spirit is working with amazing divine beings. These beings who work with us can be angels, archangels, guides, or loved ones. Most people have a group of beings that work with them on a daily basis to help their highest good. Through various religious teachings, most people believe we have guardian angels, or personal messengers, assigned by God or a higher power to protect and watch over us when we are born. Angels are believed to never have lived as human but always in spirit form. They typically will not intervene in our lives unless we ask them to.

I believe everyone has at least one guardian angel assigned to him or her. Archangels are believed to be more powerful and oversee the other angels, and they are here to serve everyone—all we need to do is ask. As a medium, I have worked with many archangels and guardian angels; they are very powerful beings of divine light to call upon. The most well-known is Archangel Michael. He is known as the protector of humanity. His courage and strength will be by your side should you call upon him.[49] I call upon Archangel Michael anytime I feel I am in need of protection, to assist with my spiritual practice, medical intuition, dream work, I am in need of courage, or for blessing houses.

---

49 Hazel Raven, *The Angel Bible: The Definitive Guide to Angel Wisdom* (New York: Sterling Publishing Co., Inc., 2006), 112.

A loved one can also choose to serve as your guardian and watch over you. My maternal grandmother serves as one of my guardians and has been with me since birth. Spending time to get to know your relatives on the spirit side of life can be very educational. You can do this intuitively or through the help of a medium. Spirit guides that come to assist you are believed to be experts in a particular area. For example, I work with Eastern and Western medicine and have different spirit guides that focus on each specialty of medicine. From what they have told me over the years, guides were in human form at one point and are now serving God from the spirit side of life. These guides and guardians in the spirit side of life agree to come into your life at certain times to help with certain lessons or situations. Some spirit guides will stay with you for your entire life, but most are specialists that come when needed and leave once the work is completed.

I have several spirit guides that teach and assist me with different types of healing, as well as one spirit guide that is my wise counsel and has been with me since birth. I have always felt his presence and energy with me, and from time to time he will come and educate and guide me when he has felt I needed to see and hear from him. From my experience, we have many divine helpers assisting us depending on what we are here to do. I have a collective crew that works with me in all areas of my life.

We have the power to get to know our guides and how they are here to assist us. I recommend connecting with them through prayers or meditations. Below is one of my favorite but simple meditations you can use to open the door to communication with your guides. Feel free to adjust it as you see fit. There is no right or wrong way to do this, so just have fun with it.

Meditation to connect with your guides or angels

- Sit in a comfortable position and close your eyes. Inhale a deep breath and hold it for the count of five. Exhale a deep breath out to the count of five.

- Imagine a beautiful white light coming down from the divine washing over the crown chakra or the top of your head. Allow this light to slowly move down over your third eye, your face, to your neck, and throat, then down through your chest and to your heart chakra. Allow this light to continue down the spine to your hips, down the arms and down the legs and out the soles of your feet. Picture this light going down into the core of Mother Earth, healing you both in a continuous flow. Allow this divine white light to nourish every cell in your body.

- Continue to breathe in this light allowing it to center and relax you.

- Now that you are more relaxed, focus your attention in your heart space. From deep within your heart, picture yourself sitting in a room. This is a sacred space for you to sit and talk with divine beings whenever you wish. What does this space look and feel like? Are there big, comfortable chairs with oversized pillows? Is the space a bit sparser and more modern?

- Allow yourself to sit in this room and just feel at peace. Set the intention to call a guide, an angel, or an archangel to come and sit and give you guidance on whatever you are trying to work through.

- Imagine this divine being walking into this room and sitting down next to you. Enjoy the unconditional love they are providing you. Ask for whatever guidance you seek, and allow yourself to be open to receive.

- When you feel this session is complete, give thanks for the connection and guidance, and watch your guide walk out of the room back to the divine.

- Slowly take deeper breaths, feeling yourself more in your physical body. Slowly move your fingers and toes and body. When you are ready, open your eyes, and smile.

I would suggest practicing this meditation consistently over the next month. It doesn't have to be every day, but as long as you're doing it at least once a week. Journal your experiences. What did your guide show you or say to you? This will allow you to evaluate how the information is presented to help you and to experience how it is manifested.

Another way to connect with your angels and guides is by setting intentions to work in your dreams. In your dream state, you are more open to interact and receive this guidance. At night, set your intention to allow your divine helpers to provide guidance to a question. I like to call specific angels and guides to be by my side as I sleep, to keep watch over me and guide me. Asking for the divine beings to work with you and protect your energy as you sleep allows for a restful sleep, feeling refreshed upon awakening, and learning in the highest divine light. I often ask to remember my dreams clearly and vividly, which makes it easier to journal upon awakening. One interesting thing I have found over the years is that Spirit will only provide bits and pieces of the answer. When this occurs, I will repeat this same intention for a few nights and journal each morning to discover more and more information until the message is fully received.

Let's say you have a decision to make about your career. Maybe you want to go to school and learn a new skill, or you want to know what field you are meant to go into, or even if you should stay where you currently are. The biggest thing to remember when you are asking for guidance is to be open to receive whatever information comes to you. I find that we try to control the divine guidance when we just need to be in a receiving state of gratitude.

Next, allow and trust that the angels and guides will step forward to assist while you sleep. When I wake up in the morning, I write down my impressions about my dreams. I describe what I saw in vivid colors, what was I feeling with my emotions, if anyone else was there, where I was, etc. I attempt to write as many details as I can. I find that I may have some insight one night, and if I work with Spirit on a particular topic for several days, the messages expand and become clearer. Remember to have patience with yourself and Spirit and enjoy the process. Always document your experiences to help with insight later. Training yourself and your work with Spirit in this way is a process, and documenting your journey is helpful to allow you not only to receive more over time but also to evaluate what the information is showing you and how it may relate to what you're experiencing in life.

Regardless of your spiritual beliefs, there does seem to be a consensus that people do some form of prayer to a higher power. Some call this higher power *God, infinite Spirit, Source, Universe, Mother Earth*, and *Father Sky* while others pray for assistance from angels and ascended masters. No matter who you are called to pray to, it is important to be respectful and express gratitude for their assistance. Some believe that prayer is a very powerful way to manifest things into your life. It is helpful to be specific to ask for what you feel you need and why. Also important is to keep your verbiage in the present tense and always end with a blessing and gratitude. Trust that your higher power will work behind the scenes to fulfill your wishes for your highest good. The trick is to allow the desire to unfold and not be attached to the outcome. Have faith it will be what is needed in divine time.

Exercise

In this exercise, you will begin to develop an active form of communication with the divine being of your choice. You may modify it as you see fit.

Sit in a comfortable seated position and say the Divine Being Prayer out loud or to yourself. Practice the Divine Being Prayer on a daily basis over the next thirty days. Keep a journal of your spirit helpers' guidance and how it manifests.

Divine Being Prayer

Oh, Great Spirit that which we call _____ (your higher power). I give thanks for your guidance, love, and protection. I call upon _____ (divine being) and I ask for _____ (your wish). I trust you will work this prayer for the highest good of all. I give thanks for your love and divine wisdom in the name and in the power of the Holy Spirit, Amen.

_____

_____

_____

_____

_____

_____

_____

_____

CHAPTER 12

WORKING WITH INTUITIVE CHILDREN

By this point you have learned how highly sensitive intuitives experience the world and ways that you can develop your natural psychic abilities while gaining a greater sense of self. You've also gained a deeper understanding of the Universal Laws and how they can aid us in living a life of intention. Through gratitude and self-awareness, we are able to become more aligned with our authentic self. But what about children? If adults can learn and develop these tools, they can also be applied and developed early in childhood.

Children are empaths and have natural abilities. I realized mine at the age of three, but it was not until I was an adult that I was able to truly grow and nurture those traits. According to a theory by Lerner et al., *positive youth development* (PYD) is important for a young person's own development, which in turn affects how the youth will contribute to the group of the community that nurtured them.

The [PYD] theory suggests that five strengths are essential for optimal youth development: competence (or a positive view of one's skills), confidence (or overall self-worth), connection (or positive bonds with people, groups, and communities), character (or respect for societal/cultural rules and sense of integrity and morality), and caring and compassion (having sympathy and empathy for others).[50]

It is invaluable to a child's self-esteem and self-worth to support and guide his or her natural abilities. In gaining a better understanding of a sensitive child's predisposition, you can foster lifelong success. This chapter focuses on children understanding their nature and provides ways to assist their personal development. The goal is to help the children in your life fully explore their abilities. Each exercise is modeled after the topics and discussions throughout the book, as well as the exercises you have completed, such as body scanning, meditation, and vision boards, all of which can be used successfully with children.

As we discovered, empaths are highly sensitive. Children who are empathic are often described as being difficult, questioning authority, and overreacting to peer interactions. They are often creative but may have difficulty having friends or may have feelings of being alone or not belonging. They tend to be oversensitive both mentally and physically, and can struggle with harsh words and overstimulation in normal physical environments. I recall as a small child making comments to my parents about being adopted. I used to tell my mother, "No one gets me." When I saw the movie, *Escape to Witch Mountain*, I remember thinking that was where I belonged, that was where my people were.

In the movie, a brother and sister named Tony and Tia were stranded on Earth after their spaceship crash-landed on Witch Mountain. The children, who looked human, had special abilities; Tia could sense or feel when something was not right, and Tony could telekinetically move objects. The siblings communicated

---

50 Bono et al., "The Power and Practice of Gratitude," 568.

telepathically, and no one around them understood how they experienced the world. They could not tell anyone the things they saw and could do.[51] As a child with so many questions about my own traits, I could relate to some of their abilities as I searched for understanding and acceptance for who I was and what I could see. Truth be told, I loved the idea of communicating telepathically and flying!

Attempting to parent a highly sensitive child can be challenging. A lot of children are highly claircognizant with a strong inner knowingness. It can be a struggle in today's society to listen to your child's guidance if it goes against your guidance. For example, your son is a highly sensitive child, and when you cook Mexican food for the family, everyone eats the food except the empath. His reason is that he feels terrible eating the spice and onions. Some might look at this as a personal preference, but these children will push back a lot harder to not eat. Or say you are listening to the radio while you are cooking and your child is sitting close by doing homework. He or she may become agitated, unable to focus because there is too much stimulation and requires a quiet room to work. The challenge for parents is to learn to trust their guidance.

One thing that benefits everyone is spending time outdoors. Children especially flourish and grow when they spend time outdoors. It is very important for a child's overall health and wellness to be outside every day regardless of the weather. Children should also spend a lot less time on electronics, which can increase the exposure to EMFs (electromagnetic fields).

Start requiring your child or children to have outside playtime every day for at least thirty minutes. Notice their energy level, focus, attention, and stress levels before and after. What did they

---

51 "*Escape to Witch Mountain* (1975 film)," Wikipedia, last modified June 5, 2020, https://en.wikipedia.org/wiki/Escape_to_Witch_Mountain_(1975_film).

enjoy and what did they not? What other activities did you all come up with together?

The opportunities are endless: gardening, playing in the dirt, riding bikes, picnics, playing in playgrounds, and swinging on swings. During summer, take your children camping. If you can't get to a campsite, set up a tent in your backyard and have an adventure. Take your child swimming. Fall is a great time to walk in the woods and look at the changing color of the leaves, make leaf paintings, harvest the garden, pumpkin carving, or going to football games. Winter is a fantastic time to make snow angels, shovel, walk in the snow, sled ride, build snowmen, or even walk around the block.

Empathic children can be easily overwhelmed and overstimulated in the harshness of our current society. Below are some exercises that may provide some much-needed tools. This can be a great way to begin to understand and apply these complex concepts to enhance you and your child's daily life.

The following exercises may assist your child/children to find a better balance of healthy foods, physical activities, and mindfulness. As with any advice or exercise, please ask your child's healthcare provider for their guidance before attempting. Also, you don't need to complete all of these exercises; just choose the ones that resonate with you and your child.

Gratitude

Just like spending time outdoors, practicing gratitude is beneficial for everyone on so many levels. Children who can learn gratitude at a young age will grow to be appreciative and will be better equipped to take on problems and issues as they develop.

- Create a gratitude calendar for the month.

- Choose a time of day (e.g., before breakfast, after dinner) where you and your child can sit down and talk about what your child is grateful for. Try to pick the same time each day to instill a routine.

- Write down one thing your child is grateful for each day. It could be more than one thing! (Examples: a funny memory, a person who made you smile, a special food).

_____

_____

_____

_____

_____

_____

_____

_____

_____

_____

Developing Self-Awareness

It is very important for a child's overall growth to develop a sense of a secure and loving environment. This can be accomplished in many ways, but for this exercise, we will help create a "happy place" in their mind. Children can utilize this exercise when they are upset or in a harsh environment and they want to leave, or when falling asleep. You may want to go through this exercise with your child to demonstrate how to do it, especially if they are younger.

- Have your child lie down or sit in a comfortable position and close their eyes.

- Tell your child to focus on a magical place where they would love to go.

- Talk your child through a visualization of what their magical place looks like. Is there sunshine and rainbows? Can they feel the sun warming their skin? Can they feel the sand between their toes? Are there dragons flying overhead? Are they riding on a horse and feeling the wind blowing through their hair? Have your child take deep breaths and breathe in those feelings of love and joy.

- Now ask your child to bring a loved one with them to their "happy place." Will their guest play, run, dance? Are they catching frogs in a pond and playing with fairies?

- Tell your child to describe their "happy place" in detail.

- Tell your child that their "happy place" is a safe place and they can visit it whenever they want. Tell your child that they are loved.

It is recommended to write down your child's experiences.

_____

_____

_____

_____

_____

_____

_____

_____

_____

_____

_____

_____

Developing Psychic Abilities

Children often do well when you make learning fun! This exercise focuses on the four "clairs": clairsentience, claircognizance, clairaudience, and clairvoyance. Choose one of the four psychic abilities you want your child to develop. You can choose more than one, if you wish.

Clairsentience

This exercise will help your child focus on their feelings in a visceral way.

- Ask your child to choose five colors.
- Ask your child to describe the colors in feelings. (Example: blue feels like water, red feels hot, yellow feels warm like the sun.)
- Ask your child to choose three shapes.
- Ask your child to describe those shapes in feelings. (Example: round feels bouncy like a ball, a star feels pointy.)

Write down their answers in your journal or in the space below.

_____

_____

_____

_____

_____

_____

_____

_____

_____

_____

_____

_____

_____

Claircognizance

This exercise will help your child learn self-awareness and distinguish between knowing how to do something versus being taught how to do something.

- Have your child close their eyes and take three deep breaths.
- Ask your child to tell you the things that are just coming into their mind (maybe they think about going to the beach, playing ball with the dog, a favorite toy).
- After each item repeat to your child and ask them to let that go and tell you what else is there.
- Repeat for two minutes.

Journal their impressions or write them below.

_____

_____

_____

_____

_____

_____

_____

_____

_____

_____

_____

_____

_____

Clairaudience

This exercise will help fine-tune your child's hearing.

- Ask your child close their eyes and name two things they hear in their environment. (Example: cars, music, people talking, birds.)

Write down their answers in your journal or in the space below.

_____

_____

_____

_____

_____

_____

_____

_____

Clairvoyance

This exercise can help your child visualize familiar objects as well as help them learn more about the object.

- Have your child choose an object they want to practice with. (Example: pictures of loved ones, toys).

- Ask your child to look at their chosen object for a few seconds, then close their eyes. They can be lying down or sitting.

- Ask them a question about the object and have your child answer with eyes closed. (Examples could be color, shape, identifying details, or patterns.)

Write down their answers in your journal or in the space below.

_____

_____

_____

_____

_____

_____

_____

_____

_____

_____

_____

_____

_____

Learning Mindfulness

Deep-breathing exercises are often very helpful to children and adults to release tension and stress within the physical body and improve the feeling of well-being. I suggest having fun with these exercises, such as over-exaggerating the sounds and movements. These exercises are inspired by relaxation techniques from the Master of Science Applied Behavior Analysis degree at Regis College.[52]

Start out by practicing these exercises for two minutes every day for one week, and then increase or change as you see fit.

Shoulder-Roll Breathing

- Sit comfortably or stand and take a deep breath in through the nose, and raise the shoulders up toward the ears.

- Breathe slowly out through the mouth and lower the shoulders as you exhale.

- Repeat lifting the shoulders up and down with the breath. Do this for three seconds in and three seconds out.

- Repeat three times. Do more or less as you feel is appropriate for your child.

Bumblebee Breathing

- Sit comfortably and gently place the tips of the pointer fingers in your ears and close your eyes.

- Breathe in through the nose for three seconds and then hum quietly as you breathe out for three seconds. When breathing out, create a bee sound, *mmmm*.

- Repeat three times.

52 "Relaxation Techniques for Kids: Benefits, Examples & Resources," Regis College, accessed June 6, 2020, https://online.regiscollege.edu/master-science-applied-behavior-analysis/relaxation-techniques-for-kids/.

Journal your child's experience or write them below.

_____

_____

_____

_____

_____

_____

_____

_____

_____

_____

_____

Learning Self-Love

This exercise will allow your child to begin to look at themselves and their life from a different perspective. Learning to love themselves and see the positive experiences all around them is important for emotional health.

- Select fun paper. (Examples could be construction paper, colorful or patterned paper.)

- Choose a topic around positive things in their life. (Examples: things they love about themselves, their strengths, positive experiences they enjoy, hobbies they love, or experiences where they felt they won.)

- Next (you or your child) write down five positive things in your child's life.

- Use crayons, markers, pencils, or paints to create a work of art.

- Discuss their answers and reinforce how much love and positive things are in their life.

_____

_____

_____

_____

_____

_____

_____

_____

_____

_____

_____

_____

CONCLUSION

My journey has been shaped by my experiences, lessons, and Spirit's presence in my life. Embracing my sensitive nature has been challenging, rewarding, and ongoing, but I wouldn't have it any other way. Learning to understand yourself and your divine birthright of intuition is a lifelong journey of self-discovery. Thank you for being part of my journey. You now have the tools to help you along your own path.

As I mentioned at the beginning of this book, my intention was for you to have an open mind to gain insights about yourself. Congratulations for taking that first step in better understanding yourself and your intuitive nature. I know the courage it takes to look at yourself from a different perspective.

I believe we are drawn to people, places, and things at the right divine time to assist whatever we are going through. It is no mistake you have read this book. Your intuition is your God-given birthright and yours to develop when you feel called to do so. By utilizing the knowledge you gained about yourself and your intuition, you are now equipped to mindfully experience the world around you. Now more than ever you need to strengthen your connection with Spirit to gain divine insight, support, and love to fully embrace life.

We are always learning new levels of self-awareness as we grow and develop. As a child, learning was more focused on the basic primal needs of food, shelter, and family. As we age, we question more about our spiritual path, why we are here, our values, and our beliefs. Taking time to explore the depth of who you are and develop your intuition daily can improve your overall perspective and well-being. I would suggest identifying what areas resonated with you in this book and explore the exercises over time to fine-tune and strengthen your abilities.

Most of us tend to get caught up in the day-to-day activities of life that we forget to care for self and our connection to the divine. Living life with a perspective of being disconnected from self and Spirit can leave you feeling as if something is missing. Remember, your spirit helpers are always with you even when you are not listening or acknowledging their presence. They will show you signs they are with you and guide you in ways similar to the examples I have provided throughout this book. Think about the times in your life when things were really tough. You have now learned how to ask Spirit for guidance. When we connect with Spirit and go within, we can find the peace and serenity we strive to find in the physical world.

After years of training in Eastern and Western medicine, reiki, hypnotherapy, spiritual healing, restructuring, medical intuition, and mediumship, I have come to the conclusion that the body, mind, and spirit are all interconnected. It is such a powerful time in our history to learn to be more aware of our mind, emotions, physical body, and connection to Spirit.

I love doing what I do and advocating for people to develop their intuition and connection with Spirit. Use the information in this book to put into action your intuitive skills to help you navigate your daily life with more confidence and success. All of the techniques in this book take time to master, so be patient with yourself. Remember to have fun and enjoy the process. Before you know it, you will be purposefully manifesting the life you desire. I wish you many blessings as you move along your intuitive journey through this magnificent world.

ABOUT THE AUTHOR

Reverend Dr. Michelle Walker DNP is a Spiritual Medium and Medical Intuitive trained in alternative and traditional medicine. Her fulfillment is working as a Doctor of Nursing, providing healthcare to the underserved as well as her work to bridge the gaps between the spiritual and physical worlds through her ministry. Walker's passion is empowering wellness by facilitating healing of the body, mind, and spirit in an aspiration to help individuals be the highest expression of themselves.

Walker received her Master of Science in Nursing from Pennsylvania State University and her Doctor of Nursing from Robert Morris University. She received her Ordination from Fellowships of the Spirit in Lilydale, New York, and is a member of The Lilydale Assembly, the largest Spiritualist Community in the world.

Since her near-death experience, Spirit has guided Walker to assist clients with their spiritual and intuitive development as well as through awareness and utilization of God-given abilities to heal ourselves. She lives in Pennsylvania.

You can learn more about Dr. Walker and her work at www.EmpoweredWellness.org

REFERENCES

Beckler, Melanie. "What Is Spiritual Awakening?" Accessed June 10, 2020. https://www.ask-angels.com/spiritual-guidance/spiritual-awakening/.

Bono, Giacomo, Mikki Krakauer, and Jeffrey J. Froh. "The Power and Practice of Gratitude" in *Positive Psychology in Practice.* Hoboken: John Wiley & Sons, Inc., 2015. https://onlinelibrary.wiley.com/doi/abs/10.1002/9781118996874.ch33.

Clear, James. "How Long Does it Actually Take to Form a New Habit? (Backed by Science)." Accessed June 9, 2020. https://jamesclear.com/new-habit.

Eden, Donna. "The Human Aura." Accessed May 26, 2020. https://www.innersource.net/em/66-handout-bank1/hbbasicprinciples/199-donna-eden-a-david-feinstein-v15-199.html.

Eden, Donna, and David Feinstein, PhD. *Energy Medicine: Balancing Your Body's Energies for Optimal Health, Joy, and Vitality.* New York: The Penguin Group, 1998.

Emmons, Robert A. and Michael E. McCullough. "Count Blessings Versus Burdens: An Experimental Investigation of Gratitude and Subjective Well-Being in Daily Life." *Journal of Personality and Social Psychology*, vol. 84, no. 2 (2003), 377–389. doi: 10.1037/00223514.84.2.377.

George, Bill. "True North: Discover Your Authentic Leadership." March 28, 2007. https://www.billgeorge.org/articles/true-north-discover-your-authentic-leadership/.

Hall, Judy. *The Crystal Bible*. Cincinnati: Walking Stick Press, 2003.

Higley, Connie and Alan. *Reference Guide for Essential Oils*. Spanish Fork: Abundant Health, 2018.

Joseph, Channing. "U.S. Navy Program to Study How Troops Use Intuition," *New York Times*, March 27, 2012. https://atwar.blogs.nytimes.com/2012/03/27/navy-program-to-study-how-troops-use-intuition/

Khoshaba, Deborah. "A Seven-Step Prescription for Self-Love." *Psychology Today*, March 27, 2012. https://www.psychologytoday.com/us/blog/get-hardy/201203/seven-step-prescription-self-love.

Lipman, Victor. "All Successful Leaders Need This Quality: Self-Awareness." *Forbes*, November 18, 2013. https://www.forbes.com/sites/victorlipman/2013/11/18/all-successful-leaders-need-this-quality-self-awareness/#d9b9c701f068.

Lockett, Eleesha. "Grounding: Exploring Earthing Science and the Benefits Behind It." August 30, 2019. https://www.healthline.com/health/grounding.

Langeveld, Irene. "Why Grounding Can be Difficult Sometimes and What to do About It." Last modified February 24, 2020. https://www.mindbodygreen.com/0-17987/why-grounding-is-difficult-for-highly-sensitive-people-what-to-do-about-it.html.

Lechner, Tamara. "10 Common Signs of Spiritual Awakening." February 13, 2019. https://chopra.com/articles/10-common-signs-of-a-spiritual-awakening.

Lexico Online. "New Age," accessed 2019, https://www.lexico.com/en/definition/new_age.

Lonegren, Sig. *The Pendulum Kit.* New York: Atria Publishing, 1990.

Luders, Eileen, Nicholas Cherbuin, and Christian Gaser. "Estimating brain age using high-resolution pattern recognition: Younger brains in long-term meditation practitioners." *Elsevier,* (April 2016): 509–510. http://www.neuro.uni-jena.de/pdf-files/Luders-NI16.pdf.

Master Choa Kok Sui. *Meditation for Soul Realization.* Philippines: Institute for Inner Studies, Inc., 2016.

Medeiros, Jenny. "Here's Why Steve Jobs Said Intuition is Absolutely More Powerful Than Intellect," *Goalcast,* June 26, 2018. https://www.goalcast.com/2018/06/26/steve-jobs-said-intuition-is-more-powerful-than-intellect/.

Merriam-Webster Dictionary. "pendulum." Accessed June 10, 2020. https://www.merriam-webster.com/dictionary/pendulum

Merriam-Webster Dictionary. "self-awareness." Accessed June 9, 2020. https://www.merriam-webster.com/dictionary/self-awareness.

Mind Tools. "What Are Your Values? Deciding What's Most Important in Life." Accessed June 9, 2020. https://www.mindtools.com/pages/article/newTED_85.htm.

Mindworks. "What Is Zen Meditation? Benefits & Techniques." Accessed June 9, 2020. https://mindworks.org/blog/what-is-zen-meditation-benefits-techniques/.

Mooney, Trish. "Subtle Body Sensing: The Impact of Flower Essences In the Human Aura." Accessed June 7, 2020. http://flowersociety.org/subtle-body-sensing.htm.

National Center for Complementary and Integrative Health. "Meditation: In Depth." Last modified April 2017. https://www. nccih.nih.gov/health/meditation-in-depth.

Orloff, Judith. "The Top 10 Traits of an Empath." Accessed May 26, 2020. https://drjudithorloff.com/top-10-traits-of-an-empath/.

Psychic Library. "clairsentience." Accessed June 6, 2020. https://psychiclibrary.com/clairsentience/

Psychic Library. "psychometry." Accessed June 6, 2020. https:// psychiclibrary.com/psychometry/

Quantum. "How Meditation Improves Group Harmony." March 8, 2017. https://quantummeditation.co.uk/meditation-improves-group-harmony.

Raven, Hazel. *The Angel Bible: The Definitive Guide to Angel Wisdom*. New York: Sterling Publishing Co., Inc., 2006.

Regan, Sarah. "The 12 Universal Laws & How to Practice Them." April 16, 2020. https://www.mindbodygreen.com/articles/the-12-universal-laws-and-how-to-practice-them.

Regis College. "Relaxation Techniques for Kids: Benefits, Examples & Resources." Accessed June 6, 2020. https://online. regiscollege.edu/master-science-applied-behavior-analysis/relaxation-techniques-for-kids/.

Sain, Helena. "A Journey through the Chakras—The Third Eye." May 3, 2018. https://www.samsaramindandbody.com/single-post/2018/05/03/A-Journey-through-the-Chakras—The-Third-Eye.

Villines, Zawn. "What is the best type of meditation?" *Medical News Today*, December 22, 2017. https://www.medicalnewstoday.com/articles/320392.

Wikipedia. "*Escape to Witch Mountain* (1975 film)." Last modified June 5, 2020. https://en.wikipedia.org/wiki/Escape_to_Witch_Mountain_(1975_film).

Wikipedia. "*Ho'oponopono*." Last modified July 5, 2020. https://en.wikipedia.org/wiki/Ho%CA%BBoponopono.

Wells, Katie. "Earthing & Grounding: Legit or Hype? (How to & When Not To)." Last modified July 30, 2019. https://wellnessmama.com/5600/earthing-grounding/.

West, John G., Nimmi S. Kapoor, N.S., Shu-Yuan Liao, June Chen, Lisa Bailey, and Robert A. Nagourney. "Multifocal Breast Cancer in Young Women with Prolonged Contact between Their Breasts and Their Cellular Phones." *Case Reports in Medicine*, Sept 18, 2013. doi: 10.1155/2013/354682.

WholisticMatters. "Cortisol, the Stress Response, and Metabolic Markers of Stress." Accessed June 9, 2020. https://wholisticmatters.com/cortisol-the-stress-response-and-metabolic-markers-of-stress/.

The Wizard of Oz, DVD, directed by Victor Fleming (1939, Culver City, CA: Warner Home Video, 2013).

Zorelle. "Getting Started with Mindfulness." February 18, 2019. https://zorellelife.com/1024/startmindfulness/.